Praise for Paul Boross

'Boross is the boss when it c
of successful, effective and i ....~ ~..~......g.'
Gavin Duffy – Dragon's Den Ireland

'Paul Boross, the business world's Derren Brown.'
Daily Telegraph

'Can't close those deals? Learn the Seven Secrets of
a Successful Business Pitch. The Pitching Bible is
great advice on sales and life.' *CNBC Bullish On
Books*

'Paul Boross has written two excellent books that
help you become more successful at pitching.'
Elite Business Magazine

'Must have books this month: Get your pitch down
with The Pocket Pitching Bible.' *Irish Tatler*

'... packed fill of good advice in bite-sized chunks for
those who want to make a stronger impact with
their presentations.' *The Irish Times.*

'William Shatner must have taken note of The Pitch
Doctor's smart tips because he delivered a
compelling performance.'
TIVU - Italian TV and Media Magazine

'If your business or personal life depends on great
communication, then you need the Pitching Bible by
Paul Boross.' *Tom Ziglar, CEO, Ziglar Inc.*

'Paul Boross is a man who can make you laugh while dramatically changing your life for the better.'
The Politics Show, BBC

'Tips for delivering engaging, collaborative and fun pitches to win business and build a network of contacts.' *Financial Mail*

'Good enough to be a beach read.'
David Lyle, CEO - National Geographic Channels

'One thing is for sure, you will greatly ImprovYourPitch with The Pitching Bible.'
Neil Mullarkey, Director at ImprovYourBiz and Co-founder of The Comedy Store Players

'Should be a standard text book at every television and film school.' *Brian Frons, President, Daytime Disney-ABC Television Group*

'Page after page, I rediscover ideas from a completely new perspective. I highly recommend it.'
Jeff Ford, Director of Programmes, Channel FIVE

'... should be required reading for anyone in business. It is simply the best advice on pitching for business. An easy read, clear and very informative.'
Andy Wood, Director a.i. Network and News at European Broadcasting Union

'A skillful mix of psychology, art, method and sheer experience to help win any pitch.'
Dr Ayan Panja, Presenter of BBC TV's The Health Show and Street Doctor

'A master class in verbal communication.'
The Daily Express

'If you want to break through as a producer read Paul's book and the secrets of getting that commission will be revealed.'
Bob Whittaker, CEO, Orion television

'The Pitching Bible is the recipe for any successful business pitch.' *Ainsley Harriott, Celebrity Chef*

'The best in the business.' *Trisha Goddard*

'Highly Recommended.' *Daily Mail*

'Jaw-droppingly simple but fabulously effective.'
Time Out

'Paul Boross is the communication expert's expert.'
Jon Briggs, voice of BBC TV's The Weakest Link

'We called in The Pitch Doctor and we estimate that we've had a 75% increase in our pitch rate as a result.'
Les Hughes, managing partner, STEEL

'Paul knows the subject inside out and understands that every great manager needs to slow down sometimes in order to go faster in the long run.'
Carl Honoré, bestselling author of 'In Praise of Slow'

Pitch Up!

Paul Boross

PUBLISHING

2013

Pitch Up!

Paul Boross

First Edition: January 2013

ISBN 978-1-908293-20-6

Published by:

CGW Publishing
B 1502
PO Box 15113
Birmingham
B2 2NJ
United Kingdom
www.cgwpublishing.com

mail@cgwpublishing.com

For Sam,

Teaching you has taught me more
than I ever knew I knew.

I hope that one day, when you are
grown up, you read this book and
tell me, "I knew all that and already
have the job of my dreams".

Contents

Pitch Up!

We live in an increasingly competitive world. More people compete for fewer resources. Employers compete for the best candidates, and the best candidates compete for the best jobs. A world of information is at everyone's fingertips, levelling the playing field. Employers no longer have to rely on what's in your CV or what a recruiter says about you, they can see your entire life story, laid out in social media updates, holiday photos and even in what you have written about other people.

In such an open, transparent world, how can you stand out and prove that you're the right candidate for the career you want?

The answer is simple.

What makes you stand out from the crowd is your ability to stand up, make a real and genuine connection with another human being and create a deep and lasting impression.

It's ironic, isn't it? The more the world becomes connected through computers and smart phones, the more we need to be connected through the most essential of human interactions.

It's often said that people buy people, and nowhere can this be more true than in recruitment. Of course, I don't mean that an employer will literally buy you, I mean that they will buy into you, your story, your potential.

If there is one message to underpin everything in this book, then this is it; that what an employer buys into is your potential. Your potential to grow, to learn and to flourish.

You are an investment, and this book is going to make it easier for people to invest in you.

This books is going to help you to get the job of your dreams.

Your Personal Brand!

Take a look in the mirror. I mean it. Put the book down and go look in the mirror.

What do you see?

Now take a closer look. A long, hard look. What do others see when they look at you?

Now look in your wardrobe. What does it tell you?

How about your social media profiles? What do they communicate about you?

If you don't yet know what a personal brand is then just think about the brands that are all around you. Mobile phones, cars, clothes, even houses and airlines, all have a personality, a brand. A set of tangible and intangible qualities which we associate with a particular company or product.

There are brands that you aspire to, and brands that you wouldn't be seen dead buying. The very best brands polarise opinion, forcing you to love or hate them. Marmite play on this in their advertising, building their branding into our everyday language to describe something that people either love or hate.

You have a brand too, your personal brand. Do people love or hate you? Or is your brand mediocre, grey, middle of the road?

Let's be clear; having a personal brand doesn't mean being crazy, wacky, in your face. It means being clear about who you are and accepting that you're not to everyone's taste.

Having a personal brand means being clear about who you are and accepting that you're not to everyone's taste

To have a personal brand means that you have to accept yourself as you are. Can you learn new skills? Of course. Can you improve your job performance? Definitely.

Can you improve the quality of your relationships? You bet. But none of those mean that you change who you are. In fact, being a learning, growing, improving person is a personal brand in itself.

The important point that I'm trying to get across to you is that before you can get the job of your dreams, you have to accept yourself, exactly as you are right now. If you can't do that, you're not ready.

Why not?

Haven't all those self help books taught you to have a big hairy goal? A master plan for your life? A compelling vision of the future, all glittery and shiny?

Well, if they have, you've been reading the wrong books. You've been reading books written by people who want to look as if they're successful, when deep down they know that they're not. The irony is that they might well be; they just don't really believe it.

Here's an analogy for you.

You set off for an interview, taking the train from your home town to London. When you change trains in Oxford, you get on the wrong train and instead of going to London Paddington, you end up in Birmingham.

You call the interviewer and say you're going to be late. They ask you where you are and you say that you're stuck in Oxford. They say, "No problem! Go to our Oxford office and we'll interview you by video conference!"

Now you're stuck. You're not where you're supposed to be, and the only thing that makes it a 'supposed to be' is that *it's what you said*.

You didn't accept where you were. You didn't accept the mistake that you made. You pretended that you weren't an idiot who can't read a sign at a station. You pretended that you were perfect. And look where it got you.

If you'd accepted where you are, you might have called the interviewer and admitted your mistake, and they might have said, "No problem! Go into our Birmingham office and my colleague will interview you."

But you chose not to give the interviewer the opportunity to help you, and you denied yourself the job. All because you were more concerned with how your mistake made you look.

Accepting yourself means that you have the courage to say, "I'm not perfect, and I like that!"

I'm not perfect, and that's my best feature!

How ridiculous, you might think. An interviewer wants someone who is perfect, don't they?

No. An interviewer is like a child with a Lego set. They don't want a boring, ready made, no thinking required recruit. They want someone who is versatile, someone with room to learn and grow.

> "There are a lot of things that are personally uncomfortable to show, especially me without makeup and completely bloated or crying. But I've realized that it's time for me to show my audience that you don't have to be perfect to achieve your dreams."
>
> Katy Perry

You're not ready-made for the job of your dreams. You will shape yourself into it. The job of your dreams isn't 'out there' waiting for you, it is inside you, waiting to be brought out by the right combination of opportunity, hard work and investment.

The job of your dreams isn't 'out there' waiting for you to find it, it is inside you, waiting to be set free by the right combination of opportunity, hard work and investment

Let's understand another important point; you don't need to develop a personal brand from scratch. You already have one.

The question is, is it serving you?

Is it aspirational?

Or is it something of an embarrassment?

Your personal brand says, "This is what I'm all about"

Perhaps the most important step that you can take in creating a compelling personal brand is to see yourself as others see you. Only by being honest with yourself will you be able to make any changes that you want.

Here's an exercise to help you to do this.

Honest Feedback

Think of the person who you get on with the least. Perhaps a colleague, a fellow student, maybe even a relative. Go to meet them, and tell them that you have a question for them. Say, "If I ask anyone else this question, they'll tell me what they think I want to hear. But even though we don't always see eye to eye, I trust you to tell me how it really is, because I know that you've got nothing to lose. Please, tell me what you think of me, what irritates you about me, and what I could do to improve myself."

And no matter what they say, thank them for their honesty. Resist the temptation to reject what they say, to disagree, to explain, to make excuses. And remember, the less you like what they say, the more valuable it is.

Recognising your brand

Still having trouble figuring out your personal brand? Well, here's an easy way to do it. If you're at home, look around you. What do you see? What you see is a mirror. The brands around you reflect you. The state of your home; tidy, messy, minimalist, cluttered, reflects you. If you don't like what you see, you have noone to blame but yourself. If you don't like it, change it.

Think about the brands that you see around you. Nike? Apple? Tesco? Porsche? Converse? Audi? Ugg? Dell? Samsung? What musicians and authors do you see? And what do they say about you?

What you see in the brands that you have chosen to place around you is what you yourself project out into the world for others to judge you by.

Your Vision

OK, having said that you shouldn't have a compelling vision, now it's time to come up with your vision. Note that a vision only makes sense *after* you have accepted yourself as you are. Only when you are honest about where you are can you ever hope to get somewhere else.

Only when you are honest about where you are can you ever hope to get somewhere else

So let's figure out where you want to get to.

What will it be like when you get there?

How will you look when you're there?

And where will you go next?

A vision cannot be an endpoint, because your life is a constantly evolving, changing journey, and so your vision cannot be of a fixed point but of a future part of that journey.

Let's create a vision.

Personal Vision

Take a blank sheet of paper. Draw yourself in the centre of it, with room around you for the different parts of your vision.

Think about the different areas of your life that you want to include in your vision. They might include, but not be limited to:

Travel   Sport   Creativity

Love   Learning   Home

People you want to meet

Qualifications   Friends

Family   Lessons learned

Spirituality   Career   Hobbies

Relationships   A 'wish list'

Health   Personal bests

Each of these areas is going to be a 'title' for an aspect of your vision.

Now take a second, larger piece of paper, the biggest you can find. A sheet from a flipchart would be ideal.

The first piece of paper is you as you are now, which is a result of you as you have been. It's time to move on from that 'you'.

Tear the paper up and set it to one side.

On the second piece of paper, draw yourself, free from the boundaries of that small piece of paper, free from the boundaries of your current role or lifestyle, free to think about your true potential.

Write the areas of your vision that you've chosen around the 'you' that you drew in the centre of the paper, placing them wherever you like and giving them each as much room as you like. Now you'll see why you need a big piece of paper.

Around each area, write a 'cloud' of ideas that support that idea and form part of it. The ideas might be existing achievements or they might be new goals and targets.

Pin the whole thing up on your kitchen wall for a whole week and add to it every day. Use different colours, draw pictures, add decorations, allow it to evolve piece by piece. Notice how, over the course of the week, you find yourself becoming more optimistic, noticing more of the good in the people you interact with.

After one week, sit down again with a blank sheet of paper. Look at your vision sheet and take a few moments to take it all in.

On your blank sheet of paper, write a summary of what you see on your vision sheet. Write it as if you are writing a profile of someone else, saying what this person is like, what their outlook on life is, What they have achieved and what their potential is.

That's your personal vision.

"Go confidently in the direction of your dreams. Live the life you have imagined."

Henry David Thoreau

Reality Check

Did your vision say anything about being a Millionaire or being world famous? Is that realistic, do you think? Can you lay out a series of steps that achieve that?

Bear in mind that real millionaires, as in genuinely successful people, rarely set out to be millionaires. They generally set out to be successful and to achieve a personal dream. Money is a consequence, not a goal.

Now that you have a vision, it's important to align your behaviour and communication with that vision. Your vision becomes a guide, a touchstone.

Finding a Touchstone

Look at your vision sheet again. What colour comes to mind? What shape? What sound?

Find an object, preferably something pocket sized, which represents your vision.

Carry it with you as much as possible.

Your vision is an important part of your personal brand because it is a statement of your direction. And when an interviewer asks you that question that they often do, about where you see yourself in five or ten years' time, you have an instant answer.

Your personal vision says, "This is where I'm headed"

Imagine that you go our for a drive in the countryside one Sunday morning. You see an interesting lane and head down it to explore. It's a dead end, but so what? You see a signpost for a cute sounding village so you take a look. All in all, you have a lovely day out.

But where did you go?

Nowhere in particular.

Where did you end up?

Back where you started.

This is great for a day out in the countryside, but it's not a good way to manage your career.

When you have a clear direction, you don't need to stop and evaluate every opportunity that comes along. You don't need to ponder on every job application or spend time on every job board. You know exactly what you're looking for and your journey will seem faster and more direct.

If you don't know where you're going, any road will get you there.

Top Tips

A recruiter buys into your personal brand. Do you want yours to be created by accident, the sum of what other people think of you? Or do you want it to be carefully crafted, a model of the career and life that you aspire to?

Not everyone will buy into your personal brand. You won't be to everyone's taste, and that's a good thing.

The job of your dreams isn't 'out there' waiting for you, it is inside you, waiting to be released by the right combination of opportunity, hard work and investment.

Create a personal vision to guide you on your journey.

Create a touchstone to always remind you of your personal vision and goals.

Be honest with yourself about where you are right now; only then will you be able to move forwards.

First
Impressions!

If you've ever watched TV's Dragons' Den, also known as 'Shark Tank' in the USA, you'll no doubt have heard one of the investors say, "I like your business, but I can't invest in you. I'm out".

Great idea. Great product. Great business case. But a singularly unimpressive and even counter-productive pitch. Arrogance. An unwillingness to listen to criticism. Rejecting the Dragons' suggestions and challenges.

Have you ever had a job interview like that?

It comes down to a simple question: Are you investable?

Some people say that first impressions are formed instantly, or in three seconds, or some other short space of time. Research from the University of Toledo[1] showed that a first impression formed in 30 seconds was consistent with an evaluation made by people with many months of interaction with a person. So while we might make an instant,reactive evaluation, after just 30 seconds we can expect that evaluation to be lasting and accurate.

I am currently appearing on a Sky TV series called School Of Hard Knocks in which we

1 http://cjonline.com/stories/062501/pro_impress ions.shtml

take young unemployed men and turn them into a rugby team in order to give them life skills and help them get a job. As the series' motivational psychologist, I am often telling them that "the way they are perceived is the way they will be received". We deliberately chose to work in deprived areas where it can be dangerous to walk down the wrong street. A young man called Dimitrios had all the swagger and attitude of a New York gangster. His fixed scowl and downward stare created an instant effect on everybody he met. When I pointed this out to him, he initially protested that it was just the way he was and that is what he had to be like to 'survive on the streets'. By mirroring his mannerisms, I explained to him the instant impression he was giving to everybody he encountered. We worked together and his whole stance and demeanour changed. He was not a dangerous lout, even though everything about him screamed 'thug'.

Remember - you never get a second chance to make a first impression.

I will tell you later what became of Dimitrios...

This works both ways, of course. You form an impression of the interviewer as much as they form an impression of you. The problem with that is obvious; if you're not sure about them, you still have the choice of whether to work around that and still accept the job. However, if they're not sure about you, then you're not in a position to make that choice.

A few years ago I made a TV series for the BBC called Speed Up Slow Down. In each episode we took someone with a disorganised life and used a variety of psychological techniques to change their lives for the better.

In one episode we worked with a musician who was well known in the 80s. His life had gone into meltdown as he was never able to get to any appointments on time. He felt that people judged him harshly just because he was late, and they should ease up on him. People had warned him about his timekeeping before, but to no effect. I had to take a different approach so we devised a plan. For the first two days, I got the producer to make appointments with him for filming, which we were deliberately late for. He got really cross with us, at which point he was ready to understand how other people felt about him. The penny dropped and, from then on, he actually became a little obsessed with being early.

Guess what happened next? He started to get interviews and job offers.

He had worn his lateness as a 'badge of honour', expecting people to overlook it and see his talents in spite of it.

At every stage of the process, and throughout this book, a key principle is to make sure that you stay in control of as many decisions as possible.

You might even say that your goal is to get the job first, and then decide if you want it.

Get the job first, and then decide if you want it

Let's go through the process, step by step, and take a look at the different first impressions that are formed along the way.

The Job Advert

In an ideal world, the job advert is scientifically written by recruitment experts who will use the precise language to attract the kind of people they want. They might say words like 'challenge', 'new' and 'dynamic' to attract someone who likes to work at a fast, competitive pace, or they might use words like 'proven', 'organised' and 'steady' to attract someone with a more mature, thorough attitude.

Imagine a movie trailer. You can just hear that voice-over guy with the gravelly voice, can't you? And which sounds more enticing of these two 'adverts'?

"What started as a global market research project soon became much, much more. In this year's funniest comedy, join Brett and Annie on a journey that takes them around the world and into each others' arms"

or...

"This film is about a boy and a girl who fall in love while visiting a couple of popular European tourist cities on some kind of contrived business trip"

If you read a job advert and think, "Ooh! That sounds just right for me!" then stop and look at the way that it's worded. Is it written to attract you? Will the reality of the job live up to that?

Here's a job advert that I've just found on a popular recruitment website:

"Are you an ambitious Account Director or Senior Account Manager looking for the next move?

If the answer is yes, then how does the opportunity of working in a vibrant, forward thinking full service creative agency sound to you?

This award winning agency are looking for an Account Director to work on a variety of exciting clients and projects, from big brand names through to some more unusual clients & sectors.

Our team is growing and we need someone to help it grow.

You will work across a variety of media and no two days will ever be the same!

You'll need to be confident, self motivated and able to lead and develop the team reporting to you. You will

> have the opportunity to take on some amazing clients, grow that business and develop your own role.
>
> The agency is big enough to bat with the big boys but small enough that you won't just be a cog in a wheel.
>
> This role is for someone who wants to make a difference."

How does that make you feel? What images does it create in your mind? What does the use of these words imply to you?

- Exciting
- Unusual

- Ambitious
- Vibrant

And finally, if this advert is a trailer for the movie, how do you think that movie is going to turn out? Just like the trailer? Or are you going to walk out of the cinema thinking that the trailer had the only good bits from the film in it, and everything else was just there to pad it out?

One possibility is that the job really is as exciting and wonderful as it sounds. But being a little cynical at times can be a useful thing, so let's take a cynical look at the advert.

What the advert says...

What the advert means...

Are you an ambitious Account Director or Senior Account Manager looking for the next move?

Duh. That's why you're looking through job adverts.

If the answer is yes, then how does the opportunity of working in a vibrant, forward thinking full service creative agency sound to you?

Vibrant = You won't have a social life any more.

This award winning agency are looking for an Account Director to work on a variety of exciting clients and projects, from big brand names through to some more unusual clients & sectors.

We like doing arty stuff instead of selling.

We won an award once; "Best kept car park".

We have one client who you'll have heard of. The rest are mainly pig farmers.

Our team is growing and we need someone to help it grow.

We want you to sell lots.

You will work across a variety of media and no two days will ever be the same!

You will be a jack of all trades.

You'll need to be confident, self motivated and able to lead and develop the team reporting to you. You will have the opportunity to take on some amazing clients, grow that business and develop your own role.

You'll have to do it all yourself with no support.

We want you to find some amazing clients.

What's amazing about the current clients is how little they pay us.

The agency is big enough to bat with the big boys but small enough that you won't just be a cog in a wheel.

We fancy our chances with the big clients but it's all down to you, really.

This role is for someone who wants to make a difference.

Get selling or you're fired.

Now I'm not for a moment suggesting that my cynical analysis is correct, I'm just saying that reality is somewhere between the two.

And if you really are an "ambitious Account Director or Senior Account Manager" then you probably already know the reality of working in a small, provincial agency.

Let's have a look at another job advert from the same site.

> "This senior level role will provide independent assurance through leading and delivering a portfolio of internal audit reviews, as to the adequacy and effectiveness of the control environment over change programmes.
>
> The senior manager will be responsible for delivering and owning a part of the audit plan. This will require in depth and hands on involvement and management of a team. The team will change regularly so the senior manger must be adaptable and have excellent people skills.
>
> The role has an extremely large change portfolio - the objective, to deliver assurance to senior management that these

programmes are being
effectively controlled.

Specialist knowledge of risk
management and audit
techniques.

Programme Management
assurance knowledge and good
business knowledge including
extensive experience of
industry best practice and
standards.

Strong service delivery
focus.

Sound Project management, to
support complex programme
reviews, using teams of
variable size and
composition, across
geographical locations.

Recent experience of
programme assurance.

Experience of risk
identification and defining
practical solutions for
management.

Evidence of proven career
track record and consistent
record of achievement"

What do the following words mean to you?

- Independent
- Specialist

- Responsible
- Evidence

Can you see how this advert is worded to attract someone who is safe, experienced, thorough, process-oriented and reliable? And can you see how that could be at odds with a possible reality of the job, which might call for moments of creativity and insight in order to solve problems?

Overall, what conclusion do you draw from your analysis of these two job adverts? One thought that I would ask you to consider is that the advert is the bait and serves two purposes. Firstly, to get as many people as possible to apply. Secondly, to get the right kind of people to apply.

Therefore, if you decide that the advert is appealing to you and that you want to apply for the job, it doesn't mean that the job is right for you, it means that the advert is right for you.

It's important to look past the advert and stay focused on the job that you want, partly for the above reasons, and partly because, in large companies, it's rarely the hiring manager who writes the advert anyway. They have teams of recruitment specialists who do that, and in large corporates, part of their remit is to position the brand and corporate values, which may or may not be relevant to the job, and may be more about aspiration than reality.

I have a simple piece of advice for you; when you're looking through job adverts, don't pay much attention to the advert itself. Concentrate more on finding jobs in the kind of company that you want to work for, and at the level that you can aspire to.

Coming back to the first advert, if you're an ambitions account manager, are you better off, in career terms, being not just "a cog in a wheel", or are you better off being a small fish in a big pond with opportunity to grow?

The first advert essentially says that they're looking for someone bigger than they are, in terms of mindset and experience. They want someone who's going to help them grow. You'll need to be the kind of person who enjoys dragging a growing business along with you, always making promises to clients that you pray the creative team can keep, and always committing to projects that, in your heart, you know will be a real challenge to deliver. If the rest of the team can live up to that challenge then that can be hugely rewarding, but if their reaction is, "For goodness sake, why have you sold that? You know we can't deliver it!" then you know that you're going to feel undervalued and frustrated very quickly.

On the other hand, taking a more junior role in a larger agency means that you have room to grow and, most importantly, people to learn from who will help you to grow. When you're the only fish in a small pond, who do you learn from? The first advert is looking for someone ready-made who doesn't need to grow, intellectually.

If you want to accelerate your career, it is very important that you have mentors. Without mentors, there is noone to show you the way forwards.

Remember. Choose the company and level first, the job description second.

Your Preconceptions

You already know lots of companies, and that biases your view of a job. Many people are drawn to working for well known companies, because they think it sounds impressive to say that they work for Microsoft, Cisco, Sony, Apple, Barclays or Unilever. But who would want to tell their friends that they work for Diageo, CRH, Glencore, Fresnillo or Antofagasta?

Who would you work for?

Work through the following list of companies and place a tick against the names that you recognise. Then count the number that you have marked.

1   HSBC Holdings

2   BP

3   Vodafone Group

4   GlaxoSmithKline

5   British American Tobacco

6   Royal Dutch Shell

7   Diageo

8   SABMiller

9   Rio Tinto

10   BHP Billiton

11   AstraZeneca

12   BG Group

13   Standard Chartered

14   Lloyds Banking Group

15   Unilever

16   Xstrata

17   Barclays

18   Reckitt Benckiser Group

19	Tesco	
20	National Grid	
21	Imperial Tobacco Group	
22	Anglo American	
23	Glencore	
24	Prudential	
25	BT Group	
26	Royal Bank of Scotland Group	
27	Centrica	
28	Rolls-Royce Group	
29	Fresnillo	
30	Scottish & Southern Energy	
31	Compass Group	
32	Antofagasta	
33	British Sky Broadcasting Group	
34	Tullow Oil	
35	Associated British Foods	
36	WPP Group	
37	BAE Systems	
38	Experian	
39	ARM Holdings	
40	Aviva	
41	Shire	

42	Pearson
43	Legal & General Group
44	Old Mutual
45	Wolseley
46	CRH
47	Reed Elsevier
48	Standard Life
49	Kingfisher
50	Sainsbury (J)
51	Morrison (Wm) Supermarkets
52	Marks & Spencer Group
53	Land Securities Group
54	Randgold Resources
55	Aggreko
56	Smith & Nephew
57	Next
58	Burberry Group
59	Petrofac
60	Capita Group (The)
61	Intertek Group
62	Johnson Matthey
63	British Land Co
64	United Utilities Group

88 Hammerson

89 Evraz Group S.A. GDR

90 Croda International

91 International Consolidated Airlines

92 AMEC

93 Admiral Group

94 Meggitt

95 Capital Shopping Centres Group

96 John Wood Group

97 Vedanta Resources

98 Serco Group

99 Melrose

100 Pennon Group

Have you been through the entire list?

How many companies have you heard of? I have to be honest and say that I have heard of 68. I couldn't even guess at what the other 32 do.

How would you feel about seeing a job advert from one of the companies that you don't recognise? Would you be put off? Would you think, "They're not a household name, so they can't be worth working for".

What if I told you that these companies were worth anything from £2.2bn to £116bn, in terms of market capitalisation? What if I told you that the list above is actually the FTSE 100, as of December 2012? Would you be interested in working for these companies now?

The Employer's Online Presence

Information is certainly the best antidote to preconceptions, and there are plenty of sources of information about companies that you might be applying to.

However, as with job adverts, websites are written to present their owners in the best possible light.

While a website will give you valuable information about a company's products, services, customers and people, other sites may give you a different perspective on things like customer service, product reliability and employee satisfaction.

Don't only rely on what a company says about itself, look at what its customers, competitors, partners and staff are saying.

You'll find some advice on how to approach this in the chapter 'Do Your Homework!'

Your CV or Application Form

So far, all of the first impressions have been to your advantage because they place you in the position of having information and deciding what to do with it. Your application is the first time that you must create a first impression, and the more people apply for a particular job, the more likely it is that recruiting managers will base their decision on a reactive first impression.

When a hiring manager has to sift through hundreds of CVs, they have to have a system for getting to the good ones, quickly. I once heard a business owner say that she received so many applications for a marketing role that she simply threw away all of the forms with spelling mistakes and poor handwriting. There was just no way that she could read every one and apply the same criteria to each.

There is no excuse for poor handwriting today, as application forms are almost always online or at the very least in electronic format. Spell checkers are a godsend to many people, but be careful for worms that the spell chequers don't catch and make sure that you proof read your application thoroughly. Ideally, get someone else to read it, because it's easy to become word blind and not see mistakes in your own work.

When you've finished your application form, put it away for an hour or two and go do something else. Then, come back to it with fresh eyes and look at it as if you're a recruiter forming a first impression. How does it look? Neat? Ordered? Untidy? Unprofessional? Engaging? Dull?

Even when the layout of the application form is prescribed by the hiring company, you can still make sure that your layout is clear and well presented, with a readable, clear font and well organised paragraphs and lists.

You can also make sure that you word your application and CV to create a first impression, with each section starting with a clear answer or positioning statement.

If the application form asks specific questions, start each answer with a very clear, one sentence summary of your answer, like a newspaper headline.

Most people think in terms of summarising information at the end, like a conclusion to an essay. However, I want you to think about the summary as being the reason for the recruiter to read the rest of what you've written.

Here are a few examples so that you can see how the headline relates to the question.

Why are you applying for this role?

I bring a breadth of experience and can hit the ground running.

My career plan to date has been to gain more experience in cloud computing, and as a recognised innovator in this field, I feel...

Can you describe a time when you used your initiative?

I identified a £2 Million p.a. cost saving by conducting my own process efficiency research.

In 2008, when I was working as...

What is your greatest achievement?

I am a published author.

At University, I worked on a research project and realised that my work had commercial appeal. I approached a number of...

Your Social Media Profile

One you've applied for a job, you're on the recruiter's radar. If you make it to their shortlist, their next step is to research you, just as you researched them. You'd better make sure you're ready for that, by tidying up your social media profiles. Look at photos, status updates, friends and connections and anything which might contradict the image that you have portrayed in your application.

Each of us has a rich, multi-faceted life, and of course no-one would want to hire a one dimensional candidate who only lives for work. However, there's a difference between having a diverse range of interests and being a potential embarrassment to an employer.

If in doubt, use this simple test. For every photo and item on your profile, ask yourself if you would be happy for your parents to see it. If not, delete it.

When the search engines keep a verbatim record of every minute of your life, you'll thank me later for getting rid of anything inappropriate now.

The Telephone Interview

A convenient way for recruiters and hiring managers to reduce the length of the shortlist is to hold telephone interviews.

One of the ways in which candidates can let themselves down in a telephone interview is poor preparation. The call is scheduled for a particular time, so there is absolutely no excuse for having the TV on, or being in a noisy environment with traffic or children screaming. Go into an office, or lock yourself in a bedroom, or even ask to borrow a friend's office or living room for the interview. Have all of your notes to hand, your application form, your research on the company and so on.

Many people treat telephone interviews as just being a 'screening call' and therefore don't take them seriously. In fact, a telephone interview is your first opportunity to control the first impression that you make, because you are able to judge the interviewer's reactions and adjust your approach accordingly. With the application form, you can't control what else is happening around the recruiter when they first read it. With a telephone call, once you've answered, the interviewer does all the talking, allowing you to judge their personality, frame of mind, mood and so on.

It's important to be yourself, but it's also important to adapt to the other person too. So what if you don't like the way they ask you a particular question? Take it in good humour, as they might be trying to test you. Your objective is to get shortlisted for a face to face interview, because by the time you get in front of the interviewer, they have already invested enough time in you that they know you can do the job, on paper, and it's all down to personality.

Some people say that you should be confident for a telephone interview. Personally, I'd say that if you're pitching an investment idea to a hard-nosed venture capitalist then yes, they probably do expect you to know your stuff. But recruiters know that interviews make people nervous. In fact, some recruiters even set the interview up to *make* you feel nervous, because they want to see the real you, not the rehearsal in front of your bathroom mirror.

Having said that, there are some useful things that you can do to prepare yourself for a telephone interview.

Warm your voice up

There are lots of good voice exercises that you can do before your interview, ranging from the type that opera singers use, through to just talking to yourself out loud beforehand. Warming up your voice makes you less likely to 'dry up' or get a crackly voice during the interview.

Smile

A smile is the result of a series of physical and mental processes, and our bodies and minds are connected together in a 'feedback loop'. Smiling really does make you feel better. For half an hour before the interview, specifically think of things that make you smile. Look through some old holiday photos, listen to your favourite music or talk to a friend who always cheers you up. When you answer the phone, the recruiter will hear your positive attitude.

Get dressed

This may sound obvious, but if you're at home, get dressed as if you mean business. You might even dress as if you're having a real, face to face interview, because the very act of dressing for work puts you in the right frame of mind for an interview.

Find somewhere quiet

Another obvious point, but if you're taking the call during your lunch break then a crowded coffee shop is not the right place for a telephone interview.

If you're at home, make sure your friends and family know what you're doing. If you're at work, can you book a slot in a meeting room that's far away from your desk? After all, making a conference call is not an unusual activity for a meeting room.

Be ready!

Not answering your phone is as bad as being late for a face to face interview. 'No signal' or a dead battery is not an excuse.

Watch my videos

Visit my YouTube channel for tips on all kinds of pitch related subjects.

www.youtube.com/user/PitchingBible

The Face to Face Interview

An interviewer will always seek to make a first impression on you, mainly because their company offices are set up for that purpose. However, before you get anywhere near the interview room, the stage is already being set.

The location of the office, the approach, the front doors, the reception area and the staff all create a first impression.

How do you feel if a company presents itself as a slick, ambitious place to work, but when you arrive, there are staff hanging around the front door, smoking, shouting and generally behaving as if they're outside a bar?

How do you feel if you walk into a dark, dusty reception area and there's no-one there, just a phone with a sign on saying 'dial 0 for reception'?

What if the sign on the phone says, 'dial the extension number of the person you are visiting'? but there's no list of numbers. How do you feel about your interview now?

How do you feel if you walk into a bright, clean reception area, the receptionist makes eye contact with you immediately, smiles, and stands up to greet you as you approach the desk?

A retailer's head office reception area will often have low, soft chairs in what feels like a 'holding pen' area, because the majority of visitors are trying to sell something to their buyers, and so the company wants to place those salespeople at a psychological disadvantage from the start.

What do you do? Do you sink into the chairs and rest your chin on your knees with the other waiting visitors? You already know that when the interviewer comes to collect you, you're going to look as elegant as a baby giraffe taking its first steps when you try to get up.

My advice is to never, ever sit down in a reception area. You'll never embarrass yourself getting up from the low chairs, you'll be able to walk across the room and greet the interviewer as they approach you, and you'll literally be 'on your toes'.

Never sit down in a reception area

However long it takes to make a first impression, the research shows that it's quick, it's accurate and it's permanent. So if you've worked hard enough to secure a face to face interview, why would you damage your chances with a poor first impression?

Be on Time

Someone you are meeting for the first time is not interested in your excuse for running late. If I'm going to an important meeting (and what meeting isn't?) I always arrive at least half an hour early, find the meeting venue and then find a café to prepare. Being late is certain to increase your anxiety, which is not a good start to an interview. Surely, a job interview should be at least worth an extra hour of your time to make sure you know where you're going and to be properly prepared?

Face Value

When you walk into a room, people will make their minds up about you very quickly, as we have already discussed. In one glance, they will assess your credibility, social status, emotional state and intentions. And, of course, your suitability for the job.

The non-verbal information that you radiate will lay the foundation for everything that happens from the moment you enter the room.

You are broadcasting information on all channels whether you like it or not, so make sure that you have a clear and realistic outcome in mind and that you understand exactly why you are attending the interview. Seriously, you might want the job, you might want something else, such as the interview practice, or to meet the interviewer so that you can pitch yourself for a different job.

91%

91% of employers[2] equate an applicant's dress and grooming with their attitude towards their potential employer.

---

2   Jobweb.com annual survey, 2002

95%

95% equate the applicant's suitability for the job with their appearance.

A global household name in the Internet market employs sales people who go and pitch their services to corporate clients. When I was helping them to develop their pitching skills, I noticed that they turned up to pitch to clients wearing torn T shirts and jeans. They said that this was part of the image they want to create, that the client should look past their preconceptions and see the value of their innovative products and services.

They said that their clients expect to see them unshaven, wearing their gardening clothes. They said, "We're that kind of company. That's our image." and they were very defensive about it.

An artist can argue until he's blue in the face that his work communicates an important message, but if the customer doesn't like it, he doesn't buy it. Beauty is indeed in the eye of the beholder.

While art should, of course, have cultural merit that transcends its commercial value, most artists do like to eat occasionally, and so the successful ones quickly learn one of two approaches to marketing. They either paint what their customers want, regardless of whether they think it's any good or not, or they paint what they want and look for the potential customers who like it. The more people don't like it, the more their work will be appreciated by the people who do like it. They polarise opinion and, in doing so, create a stronger brand and more customer loyalty.

However, that isn't what was happening at this company. The reality was that their potential customers weren't taking them seriously.

There's a trend in marketing that we could call 'anti-branding'. It includes plain packaging, social media marketing and radical brand names such as "Water" for bottled water.

Dressing like a tramp is not anti-branding, although it certainly is memorable. While they say that 'no publicity is bad publicity', it depends on what you want to be remembered for. You also have to remember that you're not pitching to be a celebrity, you're pitching for business. The criteria for appearing in a tabloid newspaper are quite different to the criteria for making a business investment.

A senior manager at the company told me of his dissatisfaction with the sales people, saying that their approach is to, "show up and throw up". In other words, they turn up at a client's offices dressed like they've just gotten out of bed on a Sunday morning and then throw data at the audience as if that was going to be enough. Nothing but charts, lists and meaningless technical data.

An old adage in sales training is, "telling is not selling".

One way of looking at it is that the sales people don't believe that they are taken seriously at a corporate level, so rather than try to compete by wearing suits and ties, they go the opposite way, as if they're teenagers rebelling against their parents. They're presenting the client with a challenge; "Respect me because of my knowledge, in spite of your preconceptions". Unfortunately, they're not teenagers and the clients are not their parents, and the result is that the client is distinctly unimpressed.

When the client decides they don't want to do business with the kind of person who doesn't bother shaving or getting dressed for a business meeting, it's no use blaming them. It's no use saying that the client is short sighted because they couldn't see beyond your image, and after all, that is your company's image. It's the way you are. Take it or leave it. Because, equally, the client can say, "Here are the people we like to do business with. These are the people we trust to support our business. These are the people we feel we can rely on. These are the people we spend our money with. Take it or leave it."

The sales people at this Internet company said, "Well if a client's going to be like that, I don't want to do business with them". Right. So if the client won't let you act like a teenager, you don't want to do business with them anyway. How mature.

I'm not saying that you always have to wear a suit, I'm saying that you have to remove your appearance as a potential barrier between you and the interviewer.

This could equally work the other way, because rapport is a sign that two or more people feel they are somehow alike. If you pitched to this Internet company in your best pinstripe suit, bowler hat and silk tie, they might equally feel that you were too 'stuffy' for them, too 'traditional', too 'inflexible'.

What we're talking about is a culture clash. Clothes are part of what marks out our social status and affiliation, and we communicate that affiliation when meeting a new client for the first time. If you're both in suits, fine. If you're both in jeans, fine. Although I might still argue that scruffy T shirts and jeans are not generally the mark of someone who is serious about his or her business. And make no mistake, a decision to hire you is a decision to invest considerable time and money in you. By all means, show that you will 'fit in', but equally show that you're a worthwhile investment.

The mismatch, the misalignment comes when one person is dressed so differently to another that they might as well be wearing different street gang insignia.

The way you look is important, not because I say so but because your potential employer will draw a conclusion from it, and on that conclusion, they will base their decision to hire you.

Why would you limit the number of people who you can pitch yourself to, simply because of what you're wearing?

Your appearance communicates with your interviewer long before you open your mouth, so make sure you're saying what you intend to say.

Stand Out from the Crowd

In my work as The Pitch Doctor, one of the most common questions that comes up is "How do I make myself memorable?"

Standing out from the crowd is actually one of the easiest things to do. Standing out for the right reasons is one of the most difficult.

Put yourself in someone else's shoes for a moment. What makes other people stand out to you? Who is the most memorable person you have ever met? And most importantly, why were they memorable to YOU?

A quality that makes you memorable is most definitely in the eye of the beholder. What is memorable to you is background noise to someone else. So therein lies our first problem.

Your challenge is actually not to stand out from the crowd, but to be memorable to the person you want to be remembered by. How do you do that? Simply by making a genuine, sincere and direct connection with that person.

I recently heard someone say that he had approached Sir Richard Branson at a charity event and asked to interview him for a book. Sir Richard asked, "What will make your book different to all the others that are out there?", and the guy replied, "Erm, I don't know. You'll be in it?"

He didn't get the interview.

And the reason? It wasn't because his answer was lame and ill thought through, even though that was true. It was because the guy couldn't differentiate himself. Now, he succeeded in interviewing many other, less famous corporate leaders for his book. For them, being interviewed for a book was different, something new. But for Sir Richard, it's something he probably gets asked to do at least once a week. In the words of Dash from The Incredibles, "When everyone's special, no-one is".

Psychologists tell us about the principles of 'primacy and recency', where our first and most recent experiences stand out to us most strongly. So that would tell you to be the first to do something. But history is littered with examples of people who were first, but were the first to fail. One hit wonders, as it were. And in any case, watch a typical episode of TV's Dragon's Den and you'll see one entrepreneur after another trying to convince the Dragons that their new product is worth investing in, just because it's new. The answer they often get is that no-one has done it before for a very good reason - because no-one needs it!

My overall advice to you is therefore to stand out from the crowd by not trying to. Don't try to be different. Don't try to be louder or brighter than your competitors. Focus on the one person you want to impress and just be yourself. Be honest, open and sincere. Tell them why you want their attention, and why you deserve it. You don't need to be confident, because the nervous energy that you build up to achieve confidence easily spills over into arrogance, and that's a guaranteed turn-off.

Finally, if you're looking for three simple tips, here they are. To be memorable, approach the person you want to be remembered by and say:

1. I really want to meet you

2. I really want you to remember me

3. And here's why...

When you've worked hard to get an interview, it can be easy to relax a little and think that the hard work is over, when in fact the most important part of the process is still ahead of you. In a competitive job market, you're not going to get every job that you apply for, so whatever happens, use it as an opportunity to improve yourself with good experience and feedback.

It's important to keep it simple and stay focused, so I've put together my five top tips for interview success to help you prepare for the interview while keeping a clear head as you walk into it.

Preparation

What do you know about the company you've applied to or the person who is interviewing you? With tools like Google and LinkedIn, you have no excuse for going into the interview unprepared. When the interviewer asks, "What do you know about us?", they're not just being polite, they're checking to see if you've done your homework.

Appearance

What's your attitude to dressing for the interview? Are you dressing to impress? To make a personal statement? To express your individuality?

If so, go back to your wardrobe and start again, asking yourself the question, is how you look really more important than getting the job? Dress to show that you take pride in yourself, that you understand the environment you'll be working in and that you've actually made an effort. When the interview opens the door, all of these positive points will be communicated within a matter of seconds without you having to say a word.

Desire

If you were interviewing people for a job, who would you rather employ – someone who acted like they couldn't care less or someone who really seemed to want the job? If you want the job, and I'm presuming that you do because you applied for it, then don't be afraid to show it. And when the interviewer asks, at the end, if you have any questions, don't be afraid to say, "Yes – Do I get the job?"

Practice

You should know what questions to expect from the interviewer, and every question they ask is carefully crafted to get the information they need. Don't think that you can 'wing it' and make it up as you go along, because you can be sure that no interviewer wants to hire someone who does that. If there are holes in your CV, don't hope for the best, ask yourself challenging questions and practice your answers. If you fall short in some areas, demonstrate your willingness to learn and take on a challenge. If there are gaps in your employment, show that you were still doing something useful with your time.

Follow up

A good interviewer will take notes and make a considered decision, but you can't reply on everyone to be as organised. As soon as you get home from the interview, write a follow-up letter and put it in the post the same day, or drop it in at reception if you live nearby. In the letter, thank the interviewer for their time, outline the main reasons why you're the right candidate and once again emphasise how much you'd like to be given the job.

If you get the job, congratulations! But if not, don't be put off. Call the interviewer and ask them for just five minutes feedback on where they feel you went wrong. It's nothing personal, there was just someone else who was a better fit for their criteria. But by showing a genuine interest in your development, you achieve two valuable things; firstly, you improve your chances of getting the next job, and secondly, you create a good impression with the interviewer who will remember you for the next position that comes up.

The Elevator Pitch

You could think of an elevator pitch as the verbal equivalent of the personal statement at the top of your CV. The good thing about an elevator pitch is that you can tailor it to the situation, and you can instantly see the reaction that it gets.

Someone once asked me, "How do I squeeze a thirty minute pitch into three minutes?" My answer was, "You can't".

Some people think of an elevator pitch as a greatly shortened pitch, cramming a life story into thirty seconds. But that's the wrong way to think of it. It doesn't help you, and it doesn't help the person you're pitching to.

Instead of trying to cram your entire pitch into as short a time as possible, I want you to change your focus. Instead of pitching to get the job, which is extremely unlikely to happen, pitch to win a chance to pitch. Your three minutes has to buy you the next thirty.

Never try to cram all of your most fabulous ideas and compelling qualities into three minutes, or into any length of time for that matter. They will simply go in one ear and out the other, and leave the recruiter feeling more resistant to your message than they were to start with.

"I have no idea what that guy just said, but he said it so quickly that now I just don't want to listen to another word."

How do you feel when a friend starts telling you something without first introducing what they're going to say? You might feel confused, disoriented, even irritated, to the point that you have to stop them and ask, "Why are you telling me this?" Until you have a 'frame of reference', it's just noise.

The more you try to cram in, the less the listener can take in, especially if you have caught them off guard. They're just not in the right frame of mind to take in your torrent of information, regardless of how passionate or excited you may be.

Instead, focus on how that initial three minutes is the trailer for the movie, the hook that leaves them saying "Call me" instead of leaving them with their heads spinning, saying "erm.. well it was nice meeting you".

"I just met this really interesting guy. We only had a couple of minutes to talk so I've asked him to come in next week to discuss his ideas in more detail."

Think of an elevator pitch as being a brief answer to the question, "Who are you and why should I talk to you?"

Here's an example...

I'm Paul Boross, also known as The Pitch Doctor. I help people and companies to be more successful by improving the quality and impact of their professional communications.

Think of the elevator pitch as a trailer for the main feature. You might even practice your elevator pitch and use it as the introduction to your main pitch, just like a newspaper headline gives you a reason and motivation to read the full story. Just think – one elevator pitch that you can use in any situation from a chance meeting, literally in an elevator, through to the introduction of a full blown interview presentation.

This approach also means that you can adapt your pitch to whatever time the recruiter gives you. If you think you have an hour but the recruiter tells you they're running late and you only have ten minutes, you need that ability to adapt. Whether you go on to deliver the rest of your pitch right there and then, or a week later, makes no difference. What matters is that you have their full attention.

When you think, like a journalist, in terms of headline, then teaser, then story, you'll be able to adapt your pitch to any situation, turning a chance meeting into an invitation to "come up and see me sometime..."

Top Tips

A first impression is made quickly and permanently, so make sure you're creating first impressions that are appropriate for the situation you're in.

An employer makes a first impression on you too, so make sure you don't judge a book by its cover and pass over a valuable opportunity.

The impression that you create isn't just made face to face; expectations are set long before by your social media profile, your CV and even a telephone interview.

Always be early for any meeting and keep on your toes by not sitting down in the reception area.

91% of employers equate an applicant's dress and grooming with their attitude towards their potential employer.

95% equate the applicant's suitability for the job with their appearance.

An 'elevator pitch' will help you to make the most of chance meetings.

Preselling!

One of the main drawbacks of using your CV to 'sell' yourself is that you wrote it, so of course it's going to present you in the best possible light. Recruiters know this, and that means that they will tend to read between the lines when they see your CV or application form.

One solution is with a portfolio of your work. This might seem obvious if you're a graphic designer or writer, but it might not be something you've thought of if your line of work doesn't seem as relevant.

You would always include your best work in a portfolio, but the difference between this and a CV is that you're able to say, "This is my best work, see for yourself", so the recruiter can judge the quality of your work for themselves.

Think about what you could include in your portfolio. What about letters? A copy of your last appraisal? Letters of thanks from clients who you have helped?

LinkedIn has the facility to make and request recommendations, so request one from each of your contacts. Copy the best ones into a document and print it for recruiters to read, and invite them to connect with you so that they can verify that they're real. It's one thing to sing your own praises in your CV, is something quite different to have someone willing to put their praise for you down in writing.

If you still don't feel that you have anything worth putting into a portfolio then start now. Think about the areas of your work where you have some real expertise and look for ways to share it. Write articles and submit them to industry magazines. Write blog posts. Conduct research using the various free survey tools that are out there, including one that's built into LinkedIn, and write a report based on the results.

Before long, you'll have an excellent collection of work which represents your skills and knowledge and which adds a new dimension to what you've put in your CV.

Ideally, also create a profile which would fit onto a single side of paper. Turn it into a PDF that you can email, and print it out to send in the post or hand over in person.

Before you meet with anyone, you can then send them your profile and portfolio, or a link to an online version, to set their expectations about you.

Top Tips

Use a portfolio of your work to show what you are capable of.

If you don't have a portfolio, create one. Write articles, conduct research, analyse research and prepare a report. Contribute to magazines and blogs. Show a recruiter that you have new insights to contribute.

Use LinkedIn's recommendations feature to collect references and testimonials.

Write a personal profile which will fit onto a single side of paper.

Send your personal profile to people who you want to meet to 'presell' yourself.

Put your personal profile online, either as a web page or on a file sharing site, and put a link to it in your email signature.

Remember the importance of a first impression, and use your profile to bias that first impression in your favour.

Social Media!

There is no doubt that social media technologies have finally taken off, thanks to the ubiquity of internet access from different platforms; computer, smartphone, even your television. As a means of sharing real time information about what you're up to, social media excels. The questions you should really be considering are therefore *what* you share, *why* and *who* with.

One of the problems with social media is that once you've published something, it's almost impossible to take it back. Almost every high profile court case now features social media in one form or other, from text messages sent by the Prime Minister to a former tabloid editor, to the intimate tweets sent by American congressman Anthony Weiner which accidentally went public instead of to the person he intended to share his private photo collection with.

In the world of social media, there is no 'undo' button.

So let's start with the most important question: Why?

Why?

Why should use use social media? Well, the chances are that you already are using LinkedIn or Facebook or something or other. But the chances are equally high that you're not using those tools with any sense of purpose other than to keep in touch with your friends and colleagues. And that is simply not going to get you the job of your dreams.

Just because you want to keep in touch with someone who you think is important doesn't mean that they see any value in keeping in touch with you. In fact, the people who you might think it's most important to be 'connected with' on social media sites are, themselves, building personal brands, and their profiles are often managed by media agencies who specialise in that kind of thing.

Virgin Mobile, the American Red Cross and Chrysler have all suffered bad publicity because of mistakes made by the agencies that manage their Twitter accounts. Maintaining an active social media presence can be very time consuming, do you really think that household name CEOs have time to do that themselves?

'Just keeping in touch' is a waste of your time, and your contacts' time too. If your contacts in high places were going to offer you a job simply by virtue of their wonderful past experience with you, they already would have done so. They are not waiting for the right moment, the opportunity of a lifetime, and if you are, you'll be waiting for a very long time.

Don't get me wrong, those opportunities are out there, but **you have to go and find them**.

Keeping in touch must be intentional, purposeful and planned.

Therefore, the purpose of using social media is twofold:

1. Build a personal brand

2. Contact people who you want to get in front of

We'll come back to how you achieve those two objectives in a moment. For now, let's turn to the second most important question.

Who?

Social media technologies are intended for one purpose; communication.

Communication is an interactive process which takes place between two or more people. Therefore, there's no point in thinking about what you want to say until you know who you want to say it to.

Who are you aiming to communicate with?

☑ Hiring managers?

☑ Recruiters?

☑ Recommenders?

☑ Door openers?

Any of those are good targets.

98% of recruiters look at your LinkedIn profile when making a hiring decision. 42% use Twitter, and 33% use Facebook.[3]

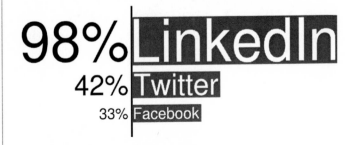

---

3   Bullhorn Reach, 2012

If you had said ex-colleagues, friends or people in high places, I would have been very cross with you.

Ex-colleagues are seeking the jobs of their own dreams, why would they help you?

Friends are people you communicate with in the pub, not using a professional medium. Keep them out of it.

People in high places are in high places because they have made a career out of ignoring people like you. It doesn't matter who you have a tenuous connection with, if they care about you, the connection wouldn't be tenuous and you'd be playing tennis with them every Tuesday morning. If you're not, then you're not important.

But wait, maybe it looks good to other people that they're linked to you?

No, it makes you look like a lonely name dropper. If people in high places would link to you, they'll link to anyone. They're linking for their benefit, not yours.

Think of it this way. Imagine that you're single and you go to a party. You see someone there who you vaguely know and who you like, very, very much. They come over and talk to you. You get on like a house on fire. They're really complementary.

They say nice things to you. They say that you should get together for a drink sometime. They take your phone number. You can't believe your luck.

During the evening, you see them going through the exact same routine with everyone at the party. Still feel special?

They are working the room to find out who is useful to them. They are figuring out what they can get out of you, not what they can do for you, and certainly not what you can do together.

The same thing happens at business networking events. Your work is really interesting. They might have some clients they can put your way. There's real synergy there. You should get together sometime and talk about some projects. And without realising it, you've given away all your good ideas and client contacts, and now you're tossed into the wind like an empty husk.

The acid test is this. Look through all the business cards that you've ever collected. Pick the top 20 most promising contacts. Look at their websites or social media profiles. Does anything look familiar? Does anything make you feel, "Hey, they could have been doing that with me! Why didn't they involve me in that?"

If they can do it without you, they don't need you

If they have done it without you, they didn't want you

What?

Create an online presence that supports your vision. Social media pages are a living CV, and while that means you can keep them updated to reflect your developing career path and experience, they also provide a permanent record that anyone with access to a search engine can find. The simple rule of thumb with the Internet is that if you think you'll eventually want to delete something, don't put it out there in the first place. Search engines such as Google aim to archive all of the world's information, and that means never deleting anything. So think of all those embarrassing photos of you as a baby that your mother likes to show your friends, and now imagine what it would be like if those photos were permanently attached to your CV.

You'll also want to keep an eye on what other people say about you and photos that they 'tag' you in, especially as the social media sites develop the technology to recognise your face and identify you in photos that people post without your knowledge.

Also, don't assume that recruiters will limit their search to only your professional profiles, so don't have a sensible LinkedIn page and a wild, party-animal Facebook page.

Would your CV say, "Hobbies: Getting drunk and taking all my clothes off in the town square?" If no, then don't put it on your Facebook page.

Similarly, after a job interview, don't Tweet "Losers. Don't know what they're missing". Again, watch the exit interviews from The Apprentice. No-one likes a sore loser.

Mind you, be careful how you celebrate your successes too. In March 2009, 22-year old Connor Riley was offered a job at Cisco, one of the world's largest Internet equipment manufacturers. She immediately Tweeted, "Cisco just offered me a job! Now I have to weigh the utility of a fatty paycheck against the daily commute to San Jose and hating the work."

It's a small world, and social media is making it smaller every day.

Top Tips

Before you engage in any kind of social media communication, stop to think about why you're doing it.

Communication is the purpose of any social media technology, so think about who you are communicating with.

Remember that once you place a photo or comment online, it's there forever.

Use social media to support your face to face networking, both as a way to make contact with people you want to meet, and to keep in touch with them.

Only share information on social media that you would share with your mother.

It's a small world, and social media is making it smaller every day.

Remember what recruiters use:

Network!

If you wait until you see a job advertised, you are already at a number of disadvantages.

- Lots of other people will apply at the same time

- All the good jobs have already gone to candidates on the 'inside'

- The job is now in the hands of recruiters

The solution is to get out there and build your network by meeting the people who are connected 'further up the tree', or closer to the source of the hiring decision. For instance, you might talk to someone who is about to lose a key member of their team but who can't advertise a position yet for contractual reasons. However, it would help them greatly if they could bring someone in on a contract basis for a handover period. Or you might talk to someone who is planning to emigrate and hasn't told their manager yet because they're hoping to get a secondment to the company's overseas office.

Another important reason for networking is to get yourself known for the right reasons, so that when a recruiter sees your CV, they think, "I remember this person, they seemed 'switched on' to me". You don't really want them to think, "I remember this person, they got drunk and fell down the stairs".

I should make it very clear that 'social networking' is not the same as networking. By all means, use social media technologies, but use them to back up your face to face networking activities. There's no substitute for getting in front of people, because ultimately they are looking to hire you, not your Facebook profile.

Get out there and meet real people. When everyone else is sitting back, waiting for the magical 'right opportunity' to arrive in their inbox, the people who land their dream jobs are out there, knocking on doors, getting ahead of the pack.

> "The most practical, beautiful, workable philosophy in the world won't work — if you won't."
>
> Zig Ziglar

Why does this old-fashioned approach work? Because very few people can be bothered to put the work into it, and because a recruitment decision is based on the recruiter meeting you, and the earlier they meet you, the better.

Keep an eye out for business networking events, and call up recruiters and HR managers and ask which events they go to. Alternatively, check the listings in your local event guide, or just search the Internet for local networking events.

There are organisations which exist only for the purpose of networking, from SME business breakfast clubs to your local Chamber of Commerce. One of the reasons that people pay an annual fee to join these kinds of clubs is that they find customers through the connections that they build.

Another reason is that they're lonely.

Why Network?

Write down your number one reason for attending a networking event:

And now write down your main measure of success when you attend a networking event, the way that you'll know that it was time well spent:

NETworkers and NOTworkers

Let's imagine that there are two types of people at a networking event.

NOTworkers

- Make a number of simple mistakes
- Say that networking is a waste of time
- Use networking events to find jobs
- Go armed with an 'elevator pitch' to tell people they meet all about themselves
- Give out lots of business cards
- Don't prepare for a networking event
- Don't follow up afterwards

NETworkers

- Do everything right
- Say that networking works
- Use networking events to make contacts
- Go to find out as much as possible about the people they meet
- Collect lots of business cards
- Prepare carefully
- Follow up on every contact made

Networking is NOT

- A way to tell people about yourself
- A way of finding jobs
- Something that you have to do

Networking IS

- An important and easy way of extending your contact network
- An opportunity to find out about people who may be of value to you
- A way of building up the contacts that will lead you to your dream job

Expert NETworkers

- Value their contact network

- Don't focus on finding targets

- Are looking for routes

- Know that their value is not in what they can do but in who they know

But there's an interesting paradox with NETworkers; they end up with lots of business cards, but that's not what they aim for. If someone boasts about how many business cards or LinkedIn connections they have, that tells you that their aim is quantity over quality. They judge their success by their own popularity, but people at networking events often aren't choosy about who they give cards to. It's very easy to go to an event with a hundred people and swap business cards with every single one, but so what? What are you going to do with those cards? Frame them and hang them on your wall?

A business card is more than a piece of paper; it's a symbol for a connection, and a convenient way to remember someone's details. It's not a trophy.

Good NETworkers go to an event with the intention of meeting lots of people, but that is not an end in itself. Their primary goal is to meet as many as possible of the *right* people, and the only way to meet lots of the right people is to meet lots of people, and to then be very selective about who you follow up with, and how.

NETworkers rarely discount a connection as worthless because they have the utmost respect for the people they meet. Instead, they apply a kind of informal grading system based not on someone's air of authority or their important sounding job title but on their ability and willingness to connect to other people. A good NETworker might even test this out during the conversation. They might meet someone who boasts that they know Peter Jones, Richard Branson, Donald Trump and so on, so they test by saying, "Ah, I'm in London on Tuesday meeting with Virgin, how do you feel about introducing me?"

If they go pale and make excuses, they're a NOTworker. If they say, "Of course, I'll pass on your details" then they're most likely leading you on and have no such intention. Good NETworkers protect the people in their network rather than spamming them with unsolicited contacts. If they say, "Well,

I could do, but I'll warn you now that he's very selective with his time. It would help if I could put a really compelling reason to him", then you've hit the jackpot, and you'd better have that compelling reason ready!

Goals

I asked you to write down your reason for attending a networking event. Was it "To find a job"? If so, you'll be looking all night. Don't get me wrong, sometimes you will go to a networking event, and everything just falls into place. The right person is there, with the right opportunity, at the right time. But it's more often the case than you'll get results from networking with nothing more complicated than good old fashioned hard work.

Your goal for attending a networking event should therefore be:

"To meet as many people as possible"

Your networking goal:
To meet as many people as possible

The key to success is that this goal is under your control, whereas finding someone ready to offer you a job is down to pure chance.

As you meet more and more people at networking events, you'll begin to get an idea of the landscape within which you're operating, the players, the people who it's good to know. You'll also meet some hangers-on, people who just like collecting business cards but never quite get round to putting you in touch with the person you want to speak to. They see their network as an asset, only to be used when they want something from someone.

Fundamentally, the purpose of networking is... well, networking. Increasing the size and quality of your contact network. It's not about collecting business cards, and it's not a competition to have the most Facebook friends. A network is like a garden; to get the most out of it, you occasionally have to do some fairly aggressive pruning.

For now, let's focus on the aspect of networking which puts most people off and enables you to get a real head start on your competitors – going up and talking to strangers.

Introducing Yourself

At a party, do you go round introducing yourself to people you don't know? Do you wait to be approached? Or do you head straight for people you already know and stick to them for the rest of the evening?

People behave in the same way at networking events. The problem is, if you only speak to people you already know then you might as well have stayed at home. The whole point of networking is to meet people you don't yet know.

The point of networking is to meet people you don't yet know

According to Dale Carnegie, everyone's favourite subject is themselves, and this is another simple way that you can differentiate yourself. I'm sure you've had conversations where you each seem to be battling to say something interesting about yourself. For many people, the purpose of listening is to be able to say something interesting and relevant. And if they can't make it relevant, change the subject and say it anyway.

In the 1988 movie Beaches, Bette Midler's character says, "But enough about me, let's talk about you, what do YOU think about me?"

Remember your purpose of attending a networking event; it's not to advertise yourself, it's to meet people and find out if they can add value to your network. You can only do that by listening to them, so as quickly as possible you need to turn the conversation round to them, and by far the most important thing to remember when you want to steer a conversation is that you have to have control of it in the first place.

If you want to steer a conversation, you have to be holding the steering wheel

You must make the approach because:

1. You get to choose who to talk to

2. You get to control the conversation

3. You get to find out what you need to know

If you wait to be approached, you're not in control of the conversation. So overcoming any nervousness that you might have about approaching strangers is key to getting results from networking. You also need to understand that it's highly likely that they are more nervous than you are.

There have been many books written about networking, and many networking 'experts' can give you their suggestions for opening lines and contrived soundbites which sound like adverts for washing powder.

"Hi, I'm John and I can impact on your bottom line through innovation and great team work!"

"Erm... hello John. I was just leaving."

Don't build up networking to be more complicated than it is. All you need to do is meet people, have a short conversation and then move on.

By far the most effective way to start a networking conversation is therefore:

1. Hello, I'm....

2. Who are you?

3. And what are you here for?

This may seem simple, yet it is very carefully structured to make networking as easy and effective as possible. Here's why.

When you make the approach and say hello, you are in control of the conversation. All you need to say is your name, and maybe just your first name to make it easy for the other person to remember.

Once you've introduced yourself, you ask a question. Asking questions is the primary way to maintain control of a conversation, and it also serves the important purpose of finding out who you're talking to!

Let's say that the other person tells you their name and job title. All good information.

Now comes to really clever part. Instead of getting into a rambling conversation about nothing in particular, you ask a very important question, which is to find out what the other person wants to achieve by attending the event.

Clever, eh?

By getting them to reveal their purpose, you find out some important information:

- Are they a good NETworker?

- Are they going to be useful for you?

- Are you going to be useful for them?

And more than that, your question encourages the polite reply, "How about you? What are you here for?"

You can now deliver your master stroke. You see, once people have overcome their fear of approaching strangers, their next problem is that they can't get away. They complain that they spent the whole evening talking to one person and may have missed some good connections. So, in answer to the question, you say, "I'm here to meet new people". In that one sentence, you tell the other person the most important thing of all; *that you won't be talking to them all night*.

You can now have a short yet meaningful conversation, and when you're ready to move on, simply say, "Well, as I said, I want to meet new people, so I'm going to let you mingle some more too. It's been really good to meet you."

As soon as you walk away, take out your pen and write some notes on the back of the person's card so that you can follow up in a way that is relevant and memorable.

But when do you swap cards? At the end of the conversation, as you say, "we must keep in touch!"

No.

At that point, the other person has already decided whether they want to hear from you again, and they can choose whether to give you a card or say they've run out. No, the time to swap business cards is at the beginning, when you say your name.

Swap business cards at the beginning of the conversation, not at the end

Remembering names

One of the things that good NETworkers do is to remember the names of the people they meet. Some people find this very difficult to do, so I'm going to give you two easy ways to do it, and I guarantee that at least one of them will work for you.

The first way is to reinforce the memory of their name, so when they tell you their name, you repeat it back to them, you mentally 'write' their name in your mind, you 'write' their name, discreetly, with your fingertip in your pocket, and you make a conscious effort to use their name as often as you can in the first minute.

An old memory trick is to make a mental image that somehow relates to the person's name. For example, if you meet Helen Wood, you might picture her as a little devil sitting amongst some trees. You have to include the person in the picture, because the purpose is to link the person's face to their name. Helen Wood, Hell in Wood. However, I would suggest that this can be helpful when you're meeting someone with a name that's easy to visualise, otherwise you'll spend so much time trying to visualise their name that you won't hear half of what they say to you.

The second way is to ask for their business card at the start of the conversation! Then, when you look back to check their job title or company you can remind yourself of their name. When you walk away, make a note of something that will help you link the name to the person, such as 'Helen Wood, purple glasses, interested in the publishing industry, email her the market research I did last year".

Breaking the ICE

Often, when you arrive at a networking event, people will have already formed into cliques, small, tightly knit groups that exclude newcomers.

How would you break into a clique?

A senior partner in an accounting practice was a master at working his way into established groups.

A junior partner wanted to learn how to achieve this miracle, so he went to a networking event and stood within earshot so that he could listen in.

What he observed was that the senior partner would approach the edge of a clique, say something, and the clique would magically open up and allow him in.

What do you think the senior partner said? What do you think his magic words were?

They were, "Hello, chaps".

That's all there was to it!

Hello chaps!

So let's put together everything you've learned about networking so far and break the ICE:

Introduce
Chat
Exit

Introduce yourself, remembering to say that you're there to meet lots of people.

Chat, about whatever you want for as long as you want

Exit gracefully, reminding the other person that you're helping them to be better NETworkers too, by giving them the opportunity to meet more people.

A Network is Like a Garden

- You have to plant seeds
- You have to pull out weeds
- You have to cultivate it
- Once planted, it grows, all by itself

They Think It's All Over...

When you get home from a networking event, email EVERY person who gave you a business card. Remind them:

- How much you enjoyed meeting them

- Why they enjoyed meeting you

- What you can do for them

- What you'd like them to do for you

And most important of all, keep in touch. After all, how do you feel about someone who you only hear from when they want something?

Your network will grow because you put effort into it. That doesn't mean a regular email asking, "Do you have any jobs?", it means the occasional email saying, "I saw this news story and thought of you", or, "I just saw your new branding on a van, it looks really good!"

Grow Your Own Network

Here's the sequence in full:

1. Say hello, introduce yourself, give a business card and ask for one in return

2. Ask, "What are you here for?"

3. Say, "I'm here to meet new people"

4. Have a brief conversation

5. Say, "Well, as I said, I want to meet new people, so I'm going to let you mingle some more too. It's been really good to meet you."

6. Shake hands and walk away

7. Make notes on the back of their card

8. After the event, follow up

The Seven Secrets of Successful Networking

- It's all about them

- Networking is not the means, it is the goal

- It really is 'who you know'

- Break the ICE - Introduce, Chat, Exit

- Everyone loves their favourite subject

- A network is like a garden

- It's all over... now the hard work begins

> "Whatever you can do or dream you can, begin it. Boldness has genius, power, and magic in it."
>
> Johann Wolfgang von Goethe

Top Tips

If you wait until the job of your dreams is advertised, you're already behind the game. Get out there and network to find the best opportunities.

NOTworkers think that networking is about finding opportunities and jobs.

NETworkers realise that the purpose of networking is to grow your network.

As your network grows, you find more routes the the opportunities you want.

You must initiate contact so that you can steer the conversation.

Swap business cards at the *start* of the conversation so that you don't have to ask at the end, and you also have a handy reminder of the person's name.

To break into a clique, just say "Hello!"

Introduce. Chat. Exit.

A network is like a garden. Take care of it and it will give you years of pleasure.

Your CV!

Your CV is probably the single most important tool that you'll use in getting the job of your dreams, because it's the one document that every recruiter expects to see. However, since you get to write it, you decide what's in it.

Of course, your CV has to be an accurate reflection of your career, because any discrepancies will certainly come out during an interview, with career limiting results.

Recruiters say that you should follow a standard format for your CV, and therefore most peoples' CVs will look very much the same.

Some people therefore figure that they should make their CV stand out with an unusual format, photos, bright colours and so on.

You might think that the recruiter's need for a standard format is based on their view that you should make their lives as easy as possible. This may of course be true.

However, many of them need your CV in a standard format because they use automated CV processing software that picks out the key information and loads it into a database. If you don't use something like a standard format, you increase the risk that something important in your CV will get missed. And, once processed, your fancy fonts and beautiful layout will be lost.

How do you then solve the problem of wanting your CV to stand out while still following a standard format?

Simple. You have more than one CV. In fact, many more.

Most people think of a CV as being a career record, a list of roles and achievements. The purpose of a CV is to communicate your career history and achievements, succinctly and clearly.

However, you are not most people. You are reading this book to give yourself an edge, and in terms of writing your CV, here it is. Your purpose for writing your CV is to have the recruiter look at it and think, "Wow! This person is perfect for the job! I've got to see them!"

The way to achieve this is to tailor your CV for each job you apply for. Now, you might think that's time consuming and surely not worth the effort, and this brings me to one of the most important points that I want to get across to you. When you are aiming for the job of your dreams, you're not going to be applying for hundreds of jobs, so you're not going to be spending hours each day customising your CV. The job of your dreams isn't just any old job, it's a special job, and worth making an effort for.

But what exactly should you customise in your CV? Let's start with the basic format and take it from there.

Headline

Your CV needs to open with a strong personal statement which positions you clearly into the role you're applying for.

"I'm looking for a role which will challenge my technical skills"

No!

Me, me, me. The recruiter doesn't care what you're looking for, they want to hear about what you're going to bring to the role.

How about this?

"An experienced designer, known for seeing traditional ideas with a fresh perspective and with a strong focus on delivering commercial results"

Experience, creativity and results. Who could ask for more?

As I said, you need to rewrite your personal statement for each job that you apply for. That doesn't mean regurgitating the job description, because your obvious attempt at flattery would be, well, obvious. Instead, think seriously about the relationship between the role and your experience. Picture yourself in the job, and imagine how the things that you do best add value to the organisation. Then write the personal statement as if it's your first appraisal.

Personal details

Your personal details contain your main contact details, including links for any online portfolios, your own website, a profile page etc. Recruitment law now prohibits your age from being used as a selection criteria, so to avoid any potential problems, recruiters often remove your date of birth from your CV, so whether you put it on or not is up to you.

Qualifications

Depending on how much work experience you have, you might put your qualifications before or after your career history.

List your academic qualifications, with dates, institution and grades achieved, listed with the highest grade, highest qualification level or most relevant first.

Career history

Some recruiters say that you should start with the most recent, others say that you should list your career history in time order. On balance, I would say that it depends on how long your career history is.

Don't limit yourself to employed positions either. List any voluntary work you've done, even on an informal basis, because it all adds to your experience of working in teams, problem solving, supporting people, directing people and so on.

If there are any gaps in your career history then include them in your CV, listing what you did and why. Even if it's something that you feel unsure about, it's better to be up-front and put it in your CV than to wait until the recruiter asks you about it. It's often more likely that the recruiter will just throw away your CV, because they have enough good candidates to not have to spend time digging answers out of you.

Hobbies

Don't make up hobbies just to make yourself sound more interesting that you are. You already are interesting!

On the other hand, if you fill your 'spare time' with computer games and pizza then you might want to think carefully about how to describe that on your CV. Recruiters aren't looking for you to have interesting hobbies, they're looking for you to be more than your work history and more than your job. They want to see that you have a life outside of work, so a statement such as, "Hobbies? I don't have time for hobbies, I just love to work!" doesn't go down well. A good employer wants to get the best out of you, not wring you dry.

References

You can save some time by putting contact details in your CV, by prior agreement with your referees of course.

The perceived importance of your referees isn't important, so don't automatically go for CEOs and celebrities. Think of people who know you well and who come across as sincere and trustworthy. It's to be expected that every referee will say something good about you, because that's the reason that you choose them as a referee! But will the recruiter find the referee credible? That's what you need to think about.

CV Tips

Update your CV regularly, after any major achievement, not only when you're job hunting, so that it's always up to date, just in case, and never comes across as being written out of desperation.

Make sure your spelling and grammar are perfect. Don't rely on a computer smell checker for this, because they don't catch words that are spelt write but in the wrong plaice. After all, you wouldn't want to

Instead, give your CV to two or three friends or colleagues and ask them to check it for you. Also ask them to tell you the overall picture that they get from it. Is it 'you'? Do you under-sell yourself? Does it sound arrogant or pompous? Take their feedback very seriously, because their first impression is an important reflection of how a recruiter will feel when they read your CV.

Finally, I've canvassed a few friends and colleagues, and they all say the same thing. Within the first five minutes of every interview they've ever been to, the interviewer asked, "Talk me through your CV, bring it to life".

Yes, your CV must be accurate and it must be realistic, but it is much more than that because during the interview, the CV is the script for your life story. When the recruiter reads that script, you want their reaction to be, "I'd like to hear more".

Therefore, always take a copy of your CV with you to an interview, even though you know the interviewer already has one. Use it practice how you're going to tell that story, how you're going to make all of your experiences fit together as if there was a plan, a strategy to lead you right up to the moment when you're sitting, being interviewed for the job of your dreams.

Top Tips

Your CV serves one purpose only; to make the recruiter want to meet you.

Keep your CV up to date all the time, not only when you're looking for a job.

Have multiple CVs for different purposes.

One CV should be in a plain, standard format that recruiters can easily load into their databases.

Rewrite your CV specifically for the job you're applying for, particularly the opening statement and the achievements in your career to date,

Have critical friends review your CV to be sure it makes the right impression.

Your CV isn't just a neutral record; it's the script for your life story.

Always be prepared to tell that story by taking your CV to the interview with you.

Do Your Homework!

In this day and age, you have absolutely no excuse for not knowing everything that there is to know about a company that you're applying for a job with. Before you even apply for a job, you can:

- Read the company's website and social media pages

- Subscribe to newsletters

- Search news sites for news about the company

- Find out if you're connected with any staff via LinkedIn

- If you are, see if they'll talk to you so that you can ask what it's like to work there

- Search the Internet for reviews and complaints

- Download and read annual financial reports

- Research the company's competitors

- Research the company's key staff and executives

Do you seriously think that the only information that a potential employer reads about you is your CV? They know that the problem with a CV is that you wrote it. But what do other people think of you? What image do you present through social media?

We live in a world of information, so you have to do two things; get hold of as much information about a potential employer as you can, and make sure that the information that they see about you is legitimate and appropriate. A photo of you being sick out of a car window is not appropriate. A photo of you at your graduation ceremony is appropriate. I think you get the idea.

For now, let's focus on the information that you need to gather and how you're going to use it.

Visit the company website and have a good read of everything that's on there. Obviously, the company will have paid marketing people to create the website, so it will present the image the company wants you to see. And that is precisely what you are looking for. Your task is not to take what you see as 'true' but to see it as a pretence, an image that the company wants to create. How does it work for you? What does it say to you? What do you think the reality could be like?

You can also visit websites where customers share their experiences of a company. The reviews don't always live up to the reputation that the company would like to portray...

HGV Category: Training Courses	From 5 reviews Write a Review	View Item
NCPLH BIIAB Licensee Course Category: Training Courses	From 1 reviews Write a Review	View Item
Category: Training Courses	From 1 reviews Write a Review	View Item
Get- Category: Training Courses	From 2 reviews Write a Review	View Item
Category: Training Courses	From 29 reviews Write a Review	View Item
Skills Category: Training Courses	From 6 reviews Write a Review	View Item
LGV Training Category: Training Courses	From 57 reviews Write a Review	View Item
The Category: Training Courses	From 2 reviews Write a Review	View Item

More companies than ever are using social media platforms to interact with customers and partners, and there have been some interesting cases of customers only being able to get long standing problems resolved by using social media, either to contact the company concerned or to generate support for their cause.

You might also compare these third party views with the company's corporate website to see how close the two messages are.

Latest Reviews in Mortgage Protection Insurance

★ ☆ ☆ ☆ ☆

"Don't go there!" Read More

★ ☆ ☆ ☆ ☆

"PPI CLAIMS" Read More

★ ☆ ☆ ☆ ☆

"THE WORST COMPANY EVER ! " Read More

★ ☆ ☆ ☆ ☆

"Disgusting unprofessional comp..." Read More

You can use platforms such as LinkedIn to research a company, and you can be fairly certain that the recruiter or employer is equally using it to find out about you.

98% of recruiters use LinkedIn, 42% use Twitter, and 33% use Facebook, and 48% of recruiters only use LinkedIn for recruitment, outside of their more traditional job sites and media advertising. So they're checking you out, and you need to check them out.

While a company's LinkedIn page is also written by its marketing team, what you will see is its connections; staff, news stories and so on. The page will show you how many employees have profiles, and they'll be ranked in order of their closeness to you in the LinkedIn network. If some are already in your network, why not contact them and ask for their advice?

The message is to do your homework, and be as thorough as possible.

There are three fundamental aspects of an organisation that you need to research; operation, culture and people.

Operation

A company's operation is made up of its products, its offices, its facilities, how it does things and how it works.

Do you like its business model? Could you feel proud of its products?

Culture

A company's culture is its unwritten rules. What's it like to work there? What's the atmosphere like? How do people work together? How do people get promotions?

People

A company's people are its greatest asset, as HR managers often say. Without people, there would be no operation or culture. What are its people like? Where do they come from? Where do they go? Why do they join? Why do they stay? Why do they leave?

Finding the job of your dreams is no accident; the more research you do, the better informed you are about where to find it

Top Tips

Finding the job of your dreams is not an accident; the more research you do, the better informed you are about where to find it.

There is more information available at every candidate and every employer than ever before. You know that a good recruiter will be doing their research on you, so you have to do the same on them.

Don't just read the organisation's own website, read consumer reviews, social media, blogs, anything that might offer you different points of view.

Research three areas to make sure that not only the job is right for you, but the organisation too.

Operation: The resources, products and business model.

Culture: The working environment.

People: Their background, where they come from, where they go if they leave.

Writing Letters!

It's standard practice to write a covering letter for a job application, and many companies specifically request one so that they can get a sense of the 'real you'.

Sometimes, when you're pitching for the job of your dreams, you'll be responding to a job advert and writing a covering letter. But at other times, there might not be a specific job to apply for and your letter will introduce a 'speculative' application or enquiry.

In either event, a covering letter will explain clearly and concisely why you are the right candidate for the job.

However, don't just stop with a letter. What else can you send? What would get the recruiter's attention, in the right way?

How about your letter, rolled up in a scroll and sealed in wax? How about a gift wrapped box, containing samples of your work?

What if you were to hand write your covering letter on the back of something relevant, like a post card if you're applying for a job in the tourism industry?

Or if you're applying for a job in hospitality, why not create your own menu?

~MENU~

TO START

Relevant Qualifications with Excellent Grades

MAIN EVENT

Initiative, Commitment and Experience, served with Enthusiasm

CONCLUSION

A Reliable, Honest and Trustworthy Deputy Restaurant Manager

A covering letter needs to say:

☑ What role you are applying for

☑ Why you are applying

☑ Why the reader should consider you

Think of a covering letter as being like the headline for a news story, or a trailer for a movie. The covering letter should make the reader want to read your application, by hooking their attention, raising their interest and then guiding them to make a decision to read through your CV – the action. Remember AIDA:

☑ Attention

☑ Interest

☑ Decision

☑ Action

Top Tips

There are three main reasons for writing a letter; to accompany an application for a job, as a speculative enquiry and to follow up.

A letter should always be specifically targeted at a person, written to and for that person and using detailed, relevant information.

Be explicit from the start and tell the reader what you want and why you're writing to them.

Make it easy for the reader to make a decision.

A letter is also your opportunity to stand out, to present your individuality.

A letter needs to be as clear and direct as possible in explaining why you're the right candidate for the job.

Remember what advertisers use; AIDA:

Attention, **I**nterest, **D**ecision, **A**ction

The Pitch!

We've finally reached what is arguably the most important point of the process, the point where you make your 'pitch' to the recruiter. This is the point at which you 'put yourself forward' or 'sell yourself', clearly articulating the reasons why you're the right candidate for the job. Bear in mind that I'm not saying the 'best' candidate, but the right one.

As I've already said, you need not concern yourself with any other candidates. The only thing that you have to do is make a clear and explicit connection between the needs of the job and your capabilities. Those needs aren't just the stated requirements of the job either; they can be implied needs such as the organisation's culture or the growth potential for the role. All of these reasons can be conveyed during your pitch.

However, pitching is a daunting prospect for many people. Not only does it involve speaking in front of an audience, which is nerve-wracking enough, it also puts you under personal and professional scrutiny. And of course, if it doesn't work out then you've lost out on an opportunity. So it's no wonder that so many people worry about pitching, yet it can just as easily be an engaging, collaborative and fun way to get your message across, win over recruiters and build that all important network of professional contacts.

The 'elevator pitch' is a perfect example of this. What most people try to do is cram their entire story into thirty seconds, thinking that if they say as many words as they can, the other person is bound to remember at least some of them. Just think how you feel when a friend starts telling you something without first introducing what they're going to say. You might feel confused, disoriented, even irritated, to the point that you have to stop them and ask, "Why are you telling me this?"

An elevator pitch needs to be a trailer for the main feature. The purpose isn't to convince the recruiter to hire you, it's to tease them and have them feel that it's worth their time to meet with you. Save your main pitch for that meeting.

Following simple tips like this actually makes all those nerves drift away, because they give you something very simple to focus on and at the same time they actually work! So to help you to get 'pitch perfect', here are my Seven Secrets for a Successful Pitch, borrowed from The Pitching Bible.

1: It's All About Them

You have your own reasons for why you want the job that you want. Whatever those reasons are, you have to remember that they are not, in themselves, good reasons for a recruiter to hire you. They are only the reasons that you want the job, not the reasons that you deserve it.

Any hiring decision is an investment in the future. Therefore, just as with any other investment, you have to present the projected return on investment for the decision maker.

Your pitch should not be, "I want, I want, I want"

Your pitch must be, "You get, you get, you get"

In short, while you are pitching because you want the job, the pitch is ultimately for the recruiter's benefit and it's them that you have to focus on. Think of everything that you're going to say from their point of view. Is it going to get the right message across to them?

Let's start by setting a goal for your pitch.

Your Goal

Let's start by setting an intention. Answer the following questions carefully.

What do you want?

Is that under your control?

What is the first step that is under your control?

How will you know when you have achieved it?

What will you see, hear and feel?

Would you take it right now if it were offered to you?

Here's another exercise for you. It will take away any nerves that you may be feeling, and it will help you to plan your pitch from a number of different perspectives, which is a very useful thing to do.

Change Your Point of View

I'd like you to remember a specific time when you presented and felt it went badly.

Many people remember their first big presentation, or perhaps something at school. When they are asked to prepare a pitch, they mentally re-run that experience.

Take some time now to mentally re-run your memory of the presentation as if you're watching a film, viewed through your own eyes. Relive exactly what you saw, heard and felt.

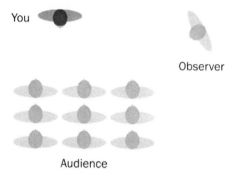

You

Observer

Audience

Remember looking out to the audience, starting just before the presentation starts to go badly and ending just afterwards. Recall the experience in as much detail as you can, making sure you have the sounds and feelings as well as what you saw. Really notice the sound of your voice and any feelings.

In between steps of this exercise, it's a good idea to take a short break. Just think about something else for a moment and then come back to the exercise.

Third, imagine yourself walking into the presentation room and sitting down as a member of the audience. Take a moment to look around you and see the other audience members.

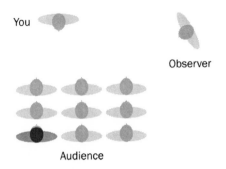

Look to the front of the room and see yourself presenting.

Watch and listen as you see yourself deliver the presentation and run a short film through from this new viewpoint. Pay attention to anything you notice at the point you thought it had "gone wrong".

Notice what you, in the audience, can see and hear. Notice how you feel about it.

Take another short break now.

Fourth, imagine yourself walking past the presentation room and stopping to peer in through the window.

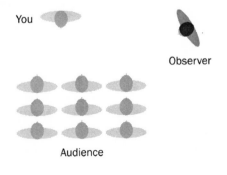

You can see both yourself presenting and yourself in the audience, and as you look from one to the other, you can see how they relate to each other. As you watch, you can run the sequence through again, and notice anything that you want to notice about it. For example, watch yourself presenting and see how the audience respond. Notice anyone in the audience who is nodding or frowning.

Take another short break now.

Now, bring what you've learned from these two new viewpoints back with you as you return to your starting point, standing at the front of the room, delivering the presentation.

Run the movie again, and this time pay close attention to how your feelings and perceptions have changed as a result of this new information.

Use this new perspective to rehearse your interview pitch.

When I deliver pitching training to companies, I ask what the team in the room know about who they are going to pitch to, and I am often surprised by how little they know about their audience.

I was working with a TV broadcaster a couple of years ago, helping a team prepare for an important pitch. I came in two days before the pitch and found out that they knew next to nothing about the main person who was going to say yes or no to the programmes they were due to pitch.

To prepare for the day, I called a contact in the business. It took me about 20 minutes. It took the people in the room about 20 seconds to exhaust their knowledge of what they knew about the man who was about to make or break their careers for the next two years. When they fell silent I told them everything I knew about the man. Former jobs, likes, dislikes, marital status, kids, hobbies. Then, to stress my point I showed them that within twelve hours of first hearing his name, I had connected with him on LinkedIn and Facebook.

The pitch wasn't about what the team wanted to sell, it was all about him.

2: By The Time You Start, It's Already Too Late

When does the pitch start?

Most people say that the pitch starts when you show the first slide, when you stand up to speak, or even when the recruiter walks into the room.

These are all wrong. The pitch starts the moment the audience buys the ticket; the moment that the recruiter first commits to listening to your pitch. That is the point at which their expectations start to form, and that is the point from which you must be able to influence them.

One of the most important things that we've talked about so far is the need for a good CV, covering letter and application form. Not to mention networking. Oh, and social networking. And pre-selling. Actually, they're all important, because they all set the scene for your pitch. Every one of those stages that you get right makes it twice as easy when you're standing there, ready to deliver your pitch, because every step that you get right makes the recruiter twice as certain that you're already the right person for the job.

But what do I mean by 'getting it right'? I'm not talking about being perfect, or reading the recruiter's mind. I mean that you put in all of the effort that you possibly can, you present yourself in a way that is true to yourself, and you don't skimp on the details.

Advertisers have, for many years, used the acronym AIDA when designing advertising campaigns:

☑ Attention – get the person's attention

☑ Interest – hold their interest

☑ Decision – get them to make a decision

☑ Action – get them to take action on that decision

It's certainly worth bearing AIDA in mind when you're designing your pitch, because you really need to plan your pitch to be the Action, not the Attention. By the time you're standing there, you already have the recruiter's attention, they're already interested and they've already made a decision to invite you in.

3: Steady, Ready, Pitch!

The recruiter has to be ready to listen before you start speaking. Get their attention and get into rapport with them, but avoid ice breakers, because they actually distract from the topic of your pitch and break rapport. Pausing before you begin is a sign of control, so take all the time you need. After all, it's your pitch for your dream job!

A lot of people say that it's important to be in rapport with the audience. Here are some key points to remember about rapport.

Rapport Checklist

Don't

☑ Stand behind a barrier such as a lectern

☑ Give all your attention to one person

☑ Turn your back on the audience

☑ Talk to the slides or whiteboard

☑ Hide in the corner

☑ Argue

☑ Lie about your intentions

Do

☑ Let your audience see you

☑ Smile

☑ Pause before beginning to speak

☑ Make eye contact

☑ Be honest

☑ Get close to the audience, but not too close

☑ Nod

☑ Keep smiling!

While it would be nice if all interviewers were straightforward, reasonable people, it's an unfortunate fact of life that some are not. For some, it's just the way they are. Others like to play the game of 'good cop, bad cop'. While it doesn't do their own reputation any good, you mustn't let it get in the way of your interview.

Whether someone genuinely disagrees with you or is just being disagreeable, here's a simple checklist to help deal with the situation.

Dealing With Disagreement

☑ When you hear something that you disagree with:

☑ Pause

☑ Notice how interesting it is that someone could have that point of view

☑ Say, "Yes, and..."

I learned a lot about this while working at the Comedy Store with the likes of Mike Myers, Paul Merton and Josie Lawrence. Comedy Store Players co-founder Neil Mullarkey now successfully trains business people in the art of 'improv' or improvisational comedy. Disagreement kills the conversation dead, whereas 'Yes, and...' keeps it alive and fosters creativity.

Overall, remember to pause and take as long as you need to prepare yourself. All good managers would rather hire someone who takes a moment to prepare for an important event than someone who rushes in and then flounders half way through for lack of preparation. All good managers know that time invested in preparation is time well spent, so you send the right messages just by pausing before your pitch!

4: Dream The Dream

Your pitch for your dream job, was created in a dream world. In order for that dream to become a reality, you need to draw the audience into that dream.

> "Lose your dreams and you might lose your mind."
>
> Mick Jagger

Drawing the audience into your dream with rich, vivid, emotional, sensory language allows you to convey far more than you ever could describe in facts, figures and 'benefits'. Bring your pitch to life and let your words carry the sights, sounds, feelings, tastes and smells of success.

As you'll discover in a few pages' time, stories bring your interview and your pitch to life in a very powerful way. If the interview is relatively unstructured, you can illustrate any example of a skill or achievement with a story. However, if the interview follows a structured, 'competency based' format, then the interview wants you to illustrate your examples with stories, so you really can't lose!

However, just telling a story of an achievement, or a time when you managed a difficult situation, isn't enough, you have to bring the story to life with the right emotions. You're not just telling the story to inform the interviewer about the facts of the situation, you are aiming to influence how the interviewer feels about the story so that it conveys the right meaning to them.

When you're talking about your aspirations, either for yourself or for the role you're discussing with the recruiter, you can use a strange quirk of language to emphasise your suitability for the role.

When people talk about good things, they talk about them in a certain, consistent way.

Good memories are
big, bright,
colourful, **close**,
sharp, **vivid** and
moving.

The same goes for bad things.

> **Bad** memories
> **are** small, dim,
> dull, far away,
> fuzzy and still.

Which do you think is best suited to an interview?

Finally, **70.9%** of corporate buyers said that they would switch suppliers on the basis that the new supplier was more fun[4].

Do you think that the same might apply to your interview?

Imagine a colleague tells you about a meeting that they just had with a manager. The colleague has made a mistake, and they're trying to get people to side with them instead of the manager. Your colleague tells you with either mock or real anger how their good points are overlooked by the manager just because they made one mistake. If you allow yourself to be drawn along by their emotions, you might easily see the situation from their point of view

---

4 According to a book that I read on guerilla marketing.

and distort the facts to fit the meaning that they intend. However, if you could take the emotion out of their words, you might think that their good points are not in dispute, it is the mistake that is the problem. You might feel confused by their reaction, and think that they should just own up to the mistake rather than trying to confuse the situation so that they can get away with it.

Your imaginary colleague might not be doing this on purpose, or they might be, but the end result is the same; they are trying to get you to distort your memory of the facts to fit the meaning that they are trying to convey to you; that they are the victim.

When you're pitching in an interview, you could tell a story about a time when you had a problem that you found a creative solution to. If you just convey the facts, it's up to the interviewer to decide if your solution was creative or not. They might even think that it would have been more important for you to stick to the rules than be creative.

Perhaps you can now see why it's so important to convey emotions as well as facts, because fact + emotion = meaning.

5: Mind Your Language

While 93% of your message may be conveyed non-verbally, there is no doubt that your language conveys the raw information that your audience needs to make a decision.

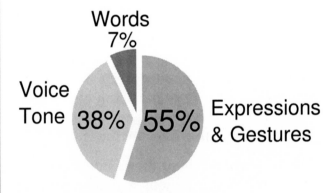

A couple of pages ago, I mentioned the importance of conveying not just facts to an interviewer but feelings and meaning.

Fact + Emotion = Meaning

Listen to the people around you and the stories they tell; about their weekend, a meeting they've just been to or a project they're working on. Listen to the way that they tell the story; the words that they emphasise, the expressions on their faces. Notice how they are trying to influence how *you* feel by communicating how *they* feel. This is the natural process of empathy, but it is also being used to manipulate your feelings about an event.

The famous research illustrated by the pie chart on the previous page shows that the overall meaning of a message is made up of three components; the words that the speaker uses, how they sound and how they look when they speak those words. A lot of people dispute the percentages, saying that words must of course make up the majority of the meaning. For example, "Hello", cannot possibly mean, "Can I have a banana?". That would be ridiculous. Oh, wait, unless you just got home from the supermarket, your friend walks in, looks at the bananas you've just unpacked, and says, with eyebrows raised and a hopeful smile, "Hello...." With that voice tone and expression, your friend could use any one of a hundred words, and the meaning would be the same.

By concentrating on how you feel about an event or achievement as you tell the story, your non-verbal communication will naturally and automatically convey the meaning alongside the words that you choose.

Competence based interviews are a structured format for getting consistent information from candidates. Practice with a friend or colleague so that you can remember examples and stories easily and confidently for a variety of situations, that illustrate different skills and strengths that you have.

An interview is different to an unsolicited pitch, because you already had to go through a selection process to get to the interview and, at least on paper, you fit the criteria for the job. However, an unsolicited pitch makes it much more likely that you have to get the recruiter's attention (remember AIDA) and overcome any cynicism on their part, cause by their 'WIIFM?' filter.

This special filter allows you to ask "What's In It For Me?" whenever you're presented with a fact or decision. You might also experience this as the "So What?" filter, the "Why Should I Care?" filter and the "Don't Tell Me What To Think" filter.

Our 'WIIFM?' filter evaluates incoming information to judge it against our own beliefs and perception of the world. It protects us from accepting other people's beliefs too readily. It prevents us from accepting new information too.

Luckily, you don't have to fight your way past the 'WIIFM?' filter, as there are two simple forms of communication which will bypass it completely.

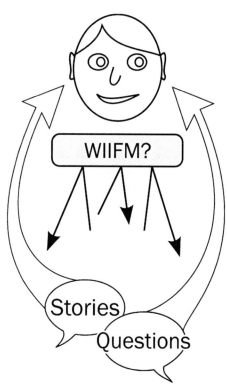

Questions

Questions are a very powerful way to convey new concepts because they build on the what the listener already knows. A question bypasses the listener's critical 'WIIFM?' filter. However, in order for the listener to make sense of the question, they must accept whatever it presupposes.

For example, what have you found to be the most valuable part of this book for you?

This question presupposes that the book has more than one valuable part, that you find it valuable and that you have already realised that value.

We hear questions when:

☑ The speaker's voice pitch rises through a sentence

☑ A sentence starts with a word such as why, when, where, how, what, which, who, if, is, could, would, will, won't, might, may, can, etc.

☑ A statement ends with a tag question, such as couldn't it, don't they, do we, can it, etc.

Asking questions during your pitch can be a very effective way to ensure the recruiter gets thoroughly engaged in the decision process.

Above all, someone who talks continuously, ramming their virtues down the recruiter's throat, will never get far.

An old adage in sales is that 'telling is not selling', and good sales people don't have the 'gift of the gab', they have excellent questioning and listening skills.

"Telling is not selling"

By listening, you get to find out about the person you're pitching to. In fact, the head of a media agency said to me that his best sales people are the ones who learn to be 'on receive' while they are pitching to clients.

Even when you're pitching, you can still be listening, judging how the recruiter is responding to you and adjusting your pitch accordingly to make sure you get across the message that you intend.

Stories

We don't communicate using factual statements alone; they are linked by a narrative, which includes characters – who did what to who – and a sequence in time, so that we can recreate the situation mentally. Imagination is a close substitute for the real thing[5], and stories are the gateway to the fundamental process of human learning.

As one person is talking, anyone listening is translating their words back into the original sensory experience. Of course, they can't translate it into exactly the original, so they are substituting their own experiences and references in order to make sense of it.

The person listening to the story puts themselves in it.

As they empathise, they 'get the message'.

---

5   Even John Lennon said, "Reality leaves a lot to the imagination".

"I get the message"

What does this mean for you?

For a start, it means that the more narrative you use, the easier you are to listen to.

Secondly, it means that the richer and more emotive your language, the more accurate the pictures are which you create in your audience's mind.

Narrative communication – storytelling - is vital, it's natural, and you already have a lot of experience in using it:

☑ Anecdotes

☑ Case studies

☑ Reports

☑ Any description of an event

It's interesting that the practice of competency based interviewing, used to make the interview process consistent and objectives, relies entirely on your ability to tell relevant stories which have the right words in; words that tell the interviewer how you analysed a situation, how you took action and how you reflected on the result that you achieved. Whether you're being interviewed in the competency style or not, having a selection of appropriate stories will definitely put you ahead of the pack.

If you're being interviewed by a HR manager, or by anyone in a large company with a well-established recruitment team, you can be fairly certain that you'll be asked competency based questions. Here are some important points for you to keep in mind in preparing to answer this type of question.

The problem or situation itself is not particularly important. What the recruiter wants to know is how you behaved and what you learned from the experience.

You can structure your answer using either CARA or STAR:

Context	Set the scene
Action	What you did
Result	The outcome
After	What you learned

Situation	The background
Task	The task or objective
Action	What you did about it
Result	What you achieved and learned

Make sure you focus on your own actions, not those of the group, even if the question asks about working as part of a team. The recruiter doesn't want to hear what other people did, they want to know about you.

But most of all, **make sure that your answers are relevant to the job you're applying for.** Everyone has bad points, of course, but if the interviewer wants to hear about them, they'll ask specifically. Otherwise, they're expecting you to sell yourself, to put your best foot forward, so make sure you're always presenting yourself in the best possible light.

A global head of HR told me that, in answer to the question, "how would you sum yourself up in one word?", one candidate once replied "messy". Guess what? She didn't get the job.

6: Say It Again, Sam

No doubt you have heard the presenter's adage, "Tell them what you're going to tell them, tell them, then tell them again". Get your message across in as many different ways that you can, and realise all of the different communication channels that you're not using; the way you dress, the way you walk into the room, what you say in your covering letter and your pitch all communicate your intention, and when all of those factors are aligned, you multiply the power of your message.

A good way to ensure that your pitch is memorable is to follow this checklist.

- ☑ Make your pitch as short as possible, but no shorter

- ☑ Have a single compelling reason for the recruiter to hire you

- ☑ Open your pitch with that reason, then provide all the supporting evidence, then conclude it with that same reason

- ☑ Use words and phrases that the recruiter has already read in your application

- ☑ Ask for the job!

7: The End... Or Is It?

Every rock star understands the importance of an encore. It's the thing that most concert-goers rave about. Some performers make the audience wait for up to an hour before being reluctantly coaxed back onto the stage for one more song... or two... or ten.

I wouldn't expect a recruiter to be shouting "More!" at the end of your pitch, but they will certainly be feeling it.

As an absolute minimum, you must send a follow up letter, reminding the recruiter of the most important points that came up during your interview, reiterating how much you want the job and reinforcing the return on investment that they'll get by hiring you. Here's an example.

Dear John,

I very much enjoyed meeting you and your colleagues this morning, and I'm writing to reiterate some of the key points that I feel really demonstrate why I feel I'm the right candidate for the role. On top of that, I enjoyed hearing about your plans for the team, and I feel very excited at the prospect of being part of that success story.

Firstly, you asked me about my experience in your specific team's area. While I do agree that my experience isn't as deep as I would like it to be, I would also add that yours is a rapidly developing area, and I believe that my ability to adapt and learn quickly is more important for you, and maybe if you hired someone with a lot of experience, they might have set views on how things should work, whereas I am very open to coming up with new ideas that will create real competitive advantage for you.

Secondly, I've worked in some very challenging environments in terms of balancing priorities, and I believe that my natural tendency to communicate very openly and directly is going to be a real asset for you in managing customer expectations.

Finally, just in case I didn't say this clearly enough already, I really enjoyed hearing about your plans for developing the team and I believe that I can make a real difference!

I look forward very much to hearing from you soon.

With best regards,

I'm not saying that this is the format that you should use, I'm saying that there are two very important points to always bear in mind about follow up letters.

1. Just sending a letter, the same day as your interview, shows that you are serious about the job

2. Reiterating the points that you want the interviewer to remember about you will greatly increase your chances of getting the job

If you have good handwriting, make the effort to write your letter by hand on good quality paper. In our digital world, it leaves a wonderful impression when someone receives personalised mail that someone has clearly taken some time and trouble over.

Many years ago, a colleague of mine had an interview with an Internet company that represented his dream job. After the interview, he hand wrote a letter to the interviewer, thanking him for his time and reminding him why he should hire my colleague. My colleague got the job, and in his first week, people were saying to him, "Ah, *you're* Fred, it was *you* that wrote the letter!" The hiring manager had apparently been running up and down the office, excitedly showing people the letter.

I was telling my son about the importance of 'thank you letters for his birthday and Christmas presents. He said "I know, Dad, you've been telling me about it ever since I was born!" I realised that I was preaching to the converted when he went upstairs to his bedroom and brought down the four already completed letters in his best 11 year old handwriting. "There you go", he said. "I realised years ago that if I sent a thank you letter, the next birthday or Christmas, the person always sent another present!"

Sam also pointed out to me that he had bought his mother a fountain pen and some lovely writing paper for Christmas so that she could "write thank you letters to her customers so that she will get more business and we can go on more holidays" The apple doesn't fall far from the tree!

Top Tips

It's All About Them: Plan your pitch from the recruiter's point of view, giving them what they need to make the right decision.

By The Time You Start, It's Already Too Late: The pitch begins the moment the recruiter starts thinking about it.

Steady, Ready, Pitch!: Get the recruiter's attention before you begin.

Dream The Dream: Convey your intentions by sharing your emotions.

Mind Your Language: Use questions and stories to bypass the recruiter's critical filter.

Say It Again, Sam: Repeat and emphasise your key messages if you want them to be remembered.

The End... Or Is It?: Make sure you follow up, as quickly as possible and with specific reference to the interview so that you can reinforce all the best points in the recruiter's mind.

Getting
Feedback!

A friend of mine went for an interview recently. The interviewer said, "Do you have any questions for us?" and my friend said, "Yes, what's your first impression of me?"

The interviewer replied, "Erm.... it's too early to tell."

I think that slightly misses the point of a first impression!

Praise is all very well but it's critical feedback that helps you to grow. Praise is reassurance. Praise lets you know that it's OK to be where you are. Praise holds you back.

Praise holds you back

Here's another bit of homework for you, which involves watching television. There's generally a 'reality TV' show on at least one of the main channels, and when contestants get evicted or voted out, they have an exit interview. Your homework is to watch those exit interviews – and maybe you can find a few on YouTube too – to work out what's going on.

Why are some people such sore losers? In The Apprentice, the exit interview is conducted in the back of a taxi cab, and I would say that probably 90% of the newly-fired candidates say, "He's made a big mistake, he couldn't see how brilliant I am, I'll make it without him, I don't need him, he'll live to regret it."

Does that sound familiar? Is it something you expect to hear from a professional? Or does it sound more like something a defeated villain in a cheap spy movie would say?

And, more to the point, have you ever said, or thought, something like that?

I do know somebody who left a well-known media corporation to start her own company. On the new website when she mentioned her old employer she jokingly wrote "that's three years of my life that I'll never get back!" Not a good way to make friends in a small world.

Get over yourself. Take it on the chin. Face up to the situation. Admit defeat. No-one likes a weasly, evasive loser who looks for anyone to blame but his or her self.

How should you cope with rejection, then?

Rejection typically happens for one of two reasons:

1. You did everything right, but another candidate was just a better fit for the job on the day.

2. You did something wrong.

What can you do about the first possibility? Absolutely nothing.

And what can you do about the second possibility? Absolutely nothing.

So what's the point, then?

The point is to learn.

The first, and most important, thing to understand about rejection is that it's not personal. After all, how could it be personal? They hardly know you!

How can rejection be personal when they don't know you personally?

Rejection means that there was nothing wrong with you, you just weren't what they were looking for. Can you ever hope to do anything about that?

Yes, you can. You can get closer to the company and the selection process. You can avoid applying for jobs that you know you're not a good fit for. And you can invest significant time and effort in preparing for the interview.

We've talked about all of this earlier on, so it shouldn't come as a surprise to you.

If the recruiter's decision is 'no', ask them for developmental feedback. You've put a lot of effort into getting as far as you did, so the least that they can do is to give you some valuable feedback.

If their answer is 'yes', then get reinforcing feedback. Ask them what they liked about you, and if they had any doubts or reservations. You're in a much better position if you find out about those doubts now, rather than waiting for your first performance review.

You need to be continually soliciting feedback from the people that you come into contact with. Recruiters all have an impression of you and an opinion about where to position you. Ask them to tell you honestly what that impression is, and if it's not in line with the impression you want to create then change something. Don't blame them, they're not the ones sending out the wrong signals!

The questions that you should continually be asking yourself are:

☑ How am I doing?

☑ What could I be doing better?

☑ What should I do next?

☑ What haven't I thought to ask?

Feedback

People often use the words 'positive' and 'negative' to describe feedback, as if it can be either good or bad. In fact:

Positive feedback = do more of this

Negative feedback = do less of this

You need both to find your way to the job of your dreams.

Both positive and negative feedback will guide you to the job of your dreams

Top Tips

Praise holds you back by making you feel good about staying where you are.

Critical feedback helps you to grow and move forward.

Rejection can't be personal because they don't know you.

Being turned down at an interview is an opportunity to get critical, constructive feedback from the interviewer. After all the hard work you've invested, they at least owe you that.

Asking for genuine feedback is a strong sign of self confidence and a desire to learn and grow – something that every good interviewer likes.

Always be asking yourself what you could be doing better.

Miss out on jobs because you didn't have the qualifications or experience, but never because you didn't make enough effort.

Getting a Promotion!

Sony's mission for many years was to put itself out of business. They realised that that was what their competitors were trying to do, and if they sat on their laurels, their competitors would ultimately win.

Therefore, if you're aiming for a promotion, take a lesson from Sony and put yourself out of a job.

To get a promotion, first put yourself out of a job

I've seen people stagnate in management positions because they had inadvertently made themselves indispensable. They often complain that their colleagues are getting promoted ahead of them, and generally that is because their colleagues are mobile. They had successors and were ready to move without upsetting the operation of the business.

The paradox is that you have to excel at your current job and at the same time show aptitude and relevant experience for a promotion. Many people find that they can't manage both, so to achieve this successfully, you have to remember one vital point; with promotion comes greater responsibility, and with responsibility comes the need to manage through relationships.

If you identify people who aspire to your current job, coach them and give them opportunities to get involved in what you're working on. Some people find this threatening, and because they don't open themselves up, they get stuck where they are. By coaching and developing others, you demonstrate the right qualities for promotion, because there is no way that anyone can successfully balance an increased workload without being able to delegate properly.

Once you've started to develop people to lift you up, your next step is to network. Get yourself in front of the right people and make your intentions clear. Don't worry about making it known that you are seeking promotion, because you are giving your employer the opportunity to get even more value from you.

A good employer would much rather develop an ambitious employee than see them leave for a competitor.

With your network in place, you could use a mentor, someone to guide you through the organisational minefield. If your employer doesn't already have a formal mentoring programme in place, go and talk to both your line manager and your HR Manager. Tell them about your aspirations and what you believe you can achieve, and tell them that you need a mentor to challenge you and help you to grow. They'll help you to find the right person. The best mentor is usually someone outside of your department, because they will have a more objective point of view, and an extra bonus is that you'll be networking out of your regular circle of connections.

And now for the single most important piece of advice that you will ever come across when aspiring to a promotion. Your employer will promote you because of what you can do, not because of what you have done.

A promotion is always an investment, never a reward

Don't beg for a reward for all the hard work you've done, all the late nights that you worked, all the projects that you completed. You did all of that in your current job on your current salary, so if anything, all you're doing is giving your employer a reason to keep you right where you are.

Instead, you need to pitch for investment. If your employer invests in you with greater responsibility or new experiences then you'll be able to deliver more and add more value.

Getting a promotion within your current employer follows all the same rules as for a job in a different organisation. You still have to build your personal brand, make the right impression, network, keep your CV up to date, pitch yourself, get feedback and so on. On top of this, the main point that you really need to focus on is the point about investment.

Aiming for a promotion has advantages over looking for external roles, although it has disadvantages too. While you already have 'inside information' and contacts, you might also run into the problem of being seen as part of the furniture by a manager who has his or her heart set on having 'fresh talent' with an external perspective. If the hiring manager is hell bent on having someone come in from a different culture then there's not much you can do about that. Or is there?

If you have taken my advice not to rest on your laurels, then you will have been regularly networking, even when you have been happy in your current role, because you never know when that dream opportunity is going to come up.

Networking exposes you to external people and ideas, and you might even actively explore secondment opportunities. The more that you can do to expose yourself to the cultures of other organisations and markets, the more easily you can overcome the 'fresh talent' obstacle by pointing out that you actually put quite a lot of effort into keeping your perspective fresh and up-to-date, and therefore the manager can have the best of both worlds; new ideas plus low risk.

Above all, whether you're looking within your current employer or externally, always be open to new opportunities. Your career path is a journey, and you're always investing in the road ahead.

> "The biggest adventure you can take is to live the life of your dreams."
>
> Oprah Winfrey

Top Tips

A promotion is an investment in your future potential.

Never ask for a promotion as a reward.

Status and power are not good reasons for a promotion; if those are the reasons then you can be sure you're being 'used'.

The best way to prepare for a promotion is to put yourself out of your current job.

Invest in people who aspire to your current job and your employer will invest in you.

Network actively, and always be open to new opportunities.

If your employer has a mentoring scheme, get on it. If not, go and ask for a mentor anyway.

A sideways move or secondment is a good chance to broaden your experience and make new contacts.

Your
Personal
Brand!

We began by talking about your personal brand. Just like any other brand, your personal brand isn't static, it's constantly evolving, as are you.

If you look back at the history of some of the most long-lived consumer brands, you'll see that their logos, colours and messages have changed, but their fundamental brand principles are still the same. Quality, innovation and service never go out of fashion.

I mentioned a young man named Dimitrios earlier. Once he became more aware of how he could change the way that people thought of him, he changed his posture and slowed down his speech. Up until that point, he had effectively lived up to the way that he thought people perceived him, without realising that he was creating that perception himself!

Dimitrios' 'thug' exterior disappeared and recruiters saw his true warm and caring nature shine. He had always dreamed of working in the fitness industry but never believed that it was possible. He now works for one of the best known health and fitness companies.

This is probably the most important point of this whole book. When someone chooses to invest their company's hard earned cash in you, they are buying into your personal brand as much as you are buying into their organisation's brand. Your brand can be an accident, the result of chance, or it can be something that you plan and work hard to build and maintain.

Working on your personal brand means being aware of everywhere that you present information about yourself, and everywhere that a potential recruiter might look to find out more about you. The best recruiters, like all good sales people, get to be the best by doing thorough research on their candidates and the market. They don't just throw CVs at a client in the hope that one will stick, they work hard to understanding their client's needs, and they carefully match candidates specifically to those needs. The hiring manager doesn't need to worry about whether the candidates can do the job, they only have to decide which one will be the best fit for their team.

And so there are two distinct stages for every interview process; getting through the recruiter and getting through the final selection. Everything in this book applies equally to those two stages, with the only difference being the reason why the interviewer is going to say, "yes" to you. The recruiter will say yes because they feel you're a strong candidate who will make them look good. The hiring manager will say yes because they feel that you are a good fit for their team.

The recruiter is investing their reputation in you, whereas the hiring manager is investing their future. And you are investing your future in them.

The job of your dreams is a step on a much longer journey, because your dreams and aspirations will change over time. When you follow my advice, you'll find yourself getting to where you want to be much faster than you had expected, and when you get there, you're not going to sit on your laurels and think that you've 'made it', are you?

Of course not. You're going to revise your plans and set your sights even higher.

The job of your dreams is a journey, and where that journey leads you is a place that you probably can't predict right now. Read any autobiography of someone who excels in any field, and they'll echo the same message, that the person knew that they would be successful, they just didn't know how, and they certainly didn't expect to be doing what they're doing now.

Did Richard Branson expect to be flying to the moon when he started his record label? Did Alan Sugar expect to be a Lord when he started selling home music systems? Did I expect to be writing this book when I was presenting my first TV show?

What successful people all have in common is a desire to move on, to achieve more, to constantly revise and refine their dreams. So in years to come, when you look back on this advice, you too might think, "Who would have thought I'd have achieved all this? Who would have said I'd be here now?"

The job of your dreams isn't out there, waiting for you to find it. It's within you, ready for you to free it. Free your dreams now, and begin your journey.

The job of your dreams isn't out there, waiting for you to find it

It's within you, ready for you to free it

Free your dreams now, and begin your journey

Believe, and you will Achieve

Acknowledgements

There are a few people who I would like to acknowledge and give a huge 'thank you' to for their part in the creation of this book.

To Sam and Henrietta - I love you - thank you for your support and inspiration.

Sam - every day you teach me something new and much of your wisdom has found its way into these pages.

To my parents, Laszlo and Helen, for their continuing love and support and for teaching me the values that have held me in good stead throughout my life.

To STEEL's Stewart Pearson and Les Hughes for their great eyes and advice.

To everyone at CGW Publishing for their continued professionalism and support.

To Emma Hughes and David Rose for the fabulous photos.

To Sue Pearson for your great artistic input.

To the colleagues and friends who have inspired and influenced me; especially Kate Benson, Owen Fitzpatrick, Brian Colbert and Dr Tim O'Brien. Also, much respect and thanks to Dr Richard Bandler, John and Kathleen La Valle and The Society of NLP.

Paul Boross, London, January 2013.

Pitch Up!

About the
Author

Paul Boross

Psychologist, author, performer, musician, NLP trainer, public speaker, corporate strategist and internationally recognised authority on communications, presentation, performance and "the art and science of getting your message across", Paul Boross is known as 'The Pitch Doctor' for good reason.

Drawing on a career that has seen him move from primetime TV and stand-up comedy to corporate training, consultancy and motivational psychology, Paul has worked with such players as the BBC, Google, The Financial Times, Royal Bank of Scotland and MTV, training executives from the worlds of business and media in a range of communication skills. He has worked with household names including Virgin chief Sir Richard Branson, TV chef and comedian Ainsley Harriott, and Sky newscaster Dermot Murgnahan.

Combining humour and motivational psychology, Paul is much in demand as a speaker at international television events, including MIPTV in Cannes, the Kristallen Swedish TV awards in Stockholm and the BCWW programming market in Seoul. He also lectures regularly for the Entertainment

Master Class, the prestigious executive education programme for the international entertainment industry.

Paul' approach to pitching and presenting - described by the Daily Express as "a master class in verbal communication" - has now been distilled into a number one Amazon best-selling book, The Pitching Bible: The Seven Secrets of a Successful Pitch, which sets out his proven techniques for "getting your message across, every time". The Pitching Bible now has a sibling, The Pocket Pitching Bible, which makes it even easier to prepare thoroughly for any pitch and get the best results.

Paul is the resident psychologist on Sky's hit series School Of Hard Knocks, now in its fourth season, with England and Wales rugby icons Will Greenwood and Scott Quinnell.

His television credits also include the primetime BBC2 series Speed Up Slow Down, a guest spot in ITV's Wannabe, advising young people on the psychology of breaking into the TV businesses; and appearances on BBC1's The Politics Show.

www.thepitchdoctor.tv

twitter.com/PaulBoross

Top Tips!

Having a personal brand means being clear about who you are and accepting that you're not to everyone's taste

I'm not perfect, and that's my best feature!

The job of your dreams isn't 'out there' waiting for you to find it, it is inside you, waiting to be set free by the right combination of opportunity, hard work and investment

Your personal brand says, "This is what I'm all about"

Only when you are honest about where you are can you ever hope to get somewhere else

Your personal vision says, "This is where I'm headed"

Get the job first, and then decide if you want it

Never sit down in a reception area

If they can do it without you, they don't need you

If they have done it without you, they didn't want you

Your networking goal: To meet as many people as possible

The point of networking is to meet people you don't yet know

If you want to steer a conversation, you have to be holding the steering wheel

Swap business cards at the beginning of the conversation, not at the end

Hello chaps!

Introduce
Chat
Exit

Finding the job of your dreams is no accident; the more research you do, the better informed you are about where to find it

Fact + Emotion = Meaning

"Telling is not selling"

"I get the message"

Praise holds you back

How can rejection be personal when they don't know you personally?

Both positive and negative feedback will guide you to the job of your dreams

To get a promotion, first put yourself out of a job

A promotion is always an investment, never a reward

The job of your dreams isn't out there, waiting for you to find it

It's within you, ready for you to free it

Free your dreams now, and begin your journey

Believe, and you will Achieve

Lightning Source UK Ltd.
Milton Keynes UK
UKOW03f1815280314

229040UK00001B/1/P